WiLL SMiTH

WILL SMITH

CHRIS NICKSON

St. Martin's Paperbacks

WILL SMITH

Copyright © 1999 by Chris Nickson.

Cover photograph by Wyatt Counts/Outline.

ISBN: 0-312-96722-5

Printed in the United States of America

St. Martin's Paperbacks edition/June 1999

10 9 8 7 6 5 4 3 2 1

ACKNOWLEDGMENTS

INEVITABLY, it would be impossible for me to complete a book without huge thanks to a remarkable agent, Madeleine Morel. On this project, I'm also grateful to John Rounds, a wonderful editor, for his faith and his prowess.

There are also large numbers of people whose support, in one way or another, helps me through. First and foremost, Linda and Graham, whose love is a rock for me, and who makes sure I actually have the time to write. Mike Murtagh, Dennis Wilken, Jonathon and Judy Savill, Paul Clark, Bob and Florence Hornberg—the friendship they all offer is felt, and appreciated. And credit must go to two more people, my parents, Ray and Betty Nickson, who gave me the impetus and encouragement to write in the first place.

Stephanie Ogle at Cinema Books in Seattle is one of the world's great resources for anything to do with film. She is not only a fount of knowledge unto herself, but she also has a seemingly endless stock of literature that proved very useful. And the helpful people at both Seattle and King County libraries deserve a word of praise, too.

As to source material, the following proved invaluable during my research: "How Will Smith Crossed Over from Hit Rapper to Hot Actor,'" in *Jet*, January 27, 1997. "Can Mr. Smith Save The World?" by Kimm Cunningham, *People*, July 15, 1996; "Will Smith Stars as Marine Pilot in Action-Thriller *Independence Day*,''; in *Jet*, July 1, 1996.

"Will and Martin," *Vibe*, April 1995. "Box Office Prince," by Allison Samuels and Karen Schoemer, *Newsweek*, July 22, 1996. "Martin Lawrence, Will Smith Star in Hot Movie *Bad Boys*," in *Jet*, May 1 1995. "Six Degrees of Trepidation," by Geoff Gordon, *The Advocate*, February 8, 1994. "Can Will Smith Play on Park Avenue?" by Meredith Berkman, *Entertainment Weekly*, December 24, 1993. "Will Smith" by Michael Segell, *Cosmopolitan*, October 1993. "Will Smith Uses Christmas Show ...." *Jet*. "Philly's Flip, Hip Will Smith Takes on Hollywood as TV's Fresh Prince," by Jeannie Park, *People*, September 24, 1990. "No Nightmares for DJ Jazzy Jeff and the Fresh Prince," by Jeffrey Ressner, *Rolling Stone* 1989. "Rap Star Finds TV Fame as 'Fresh Prince of Bel Air,' " *Jet*, 1990. "Will Smith," by Mary Murphy, *TV Guide*, September 29, 1990. "Rap'n'Rhyme with the Prince of Prime Time," by Mary Murphy, *TV Guide*, October 13, 1990. "Will Power: From Fresh Prince to Hollywood Royalty," by Jessica Shaw, *Entertainment Weekly*, June 20, 1997. "Mister Smith Goes to Stardom," by Gregory Cerio, *People*, July 22, 1996. "Will Smith Settles Down and Gets Real," by Gordon Dillow, *TV Guide*, January 28, 1993. "Will Power," by Cindy Pearlman, *Cinescape*, November/December, 1996. "Angels on Her Shoulders," by Dennis Henslet, *Movieline*, December 1996. "Making Superstardom and Love Work," by Lynn Norment, *Ebony*, September 1997. "Iron Will," by Stephen Rebello, *Premiere* (UK), August 1997. "Smith and Jones," by Rupert Howe, *Neon*, August 1997. "Will Smith Saves the Planet," by Gerri Hirshey, *GQ*, June 1997. "Will Smith," by Lynn Norment, *Ebony* August 1996. "The Future's Bright, the Future's Black," by Anwar Brett, *Film Review*, September 1997. "Mr. Jones, I Presume," by Susan Granger, *Film Review Special*, 1997. "Alias Smith and Jones," by Nigel Floyd, *SFX*, August 1997. "Smith & Jones," by David Eimer, *Total Film*, September 1997. "Mr. Smith Takes a Bride" by Alex Tresniowski, Jennifer Mendelsohn, Gerald Burstyn, Tom Cunneff, Craig Tomashoff, and Jennifer Longley, *People*, January 19, 1998. "The Thinking Woman's Actress" by bell hooks, *Essence*, March 1998. "The Fresh King," by Mike Sager, *Vibe*, September, 1998.

INTRODUCTION

FOR years, people assert, Hollywood has been looking for a crossover black star, an African-American actor who could have huge appeal to a white audience. In Sidney Poitier they could have had him, but the time and the racial climate wasn't yet right. Then with Denzel Washington the timing was good, and there's no doubt he has the looks, the talent, and even the acceptance; the only problem is that he hasn't made a blockbuster hit—one of those films that becomes the all-time top ten money-makers and embeds itself and its stars (for better or worse) in the national consciousness.

Just six years ago, no one could have confidently predicted that the breakthrough star would be Will Smith. By then he'd already enjoyed a multi-platinum career in music, as part of the hip-hop duo DJ Jazzy Jeff and the Fresh Prince, earning two Grammys along the way—including the first Grammy ever given to a rap group. He'd made the transition from concert stage to small screen, starring in "The Fresh Prince of Bel Air," which, while generally sticking to established sitcom precepts, actually managed to draw in that elusive, magical younger demographic that seems to excite television programmers.

He'd even dipped his toes into the waters of film, with a very small supporting role in the gritty movie *Where The Day Takes You,* which never had a chance of being a hit, let alone a megahit.

There was no question that Will was brimming over with confidence and ambition. Or that he had plenty of raw talent. But though he had natural comic timing, his acting on TV still left a lot to be desired. The potential was there, but fulfilling it was going to take a lot of work—and a healthy dose of luck.

But neither of those things was a stranger to Will. He had a workaholic's attitude to life—do it all now, play later—a drive that kept pushing him to ultimate success, and a habit of being in the right place at the right time. It was a combination of factors that wasn't going to hurt his advancement up the ladder of stardom.

Not many actors have made successful transitions from television to movies. In fact, the few who've managed it well have been comics—Tom Hanks, Jim Carrey. Once established in Hollywood, they've been able to expand what they do. Most, in making the jump to the larger screen, have fallen flat on their faces.

Will knew this; he understood it innately, it seemed, and he devised his own strategy to take himself to the top. Call it a series of baby steps, if you like. From the crawling of *Where The Day Takes You*, he moved to a teetering walk in *Made In America*, then impressed everyone by showing another of his facets in *Six Degrees Of Separation*, exhibiting a range well beyond comedy. And he did it all while holding firmly onto the anchor of "Fresh Prince," still performing wonderfully in the ratings. There he was definitely a star, the biggest African-American on television since Bill Cosby. He had a show that appealed to teens of *all* races, that offered role models and showed a way that family life could still be lived in the nineties.

Will's next cinematic step was the big one, starring in *Bad Boys* with another black comedian, Martin Lawrence. It was an action picture with a funny edge, not a million miles from the *Lethal Weapon* series that had done so well at the box office. Financially, though, *Bad Boys* outstripped its inspirations, grossing over $200 million internationally— enough to vault Will into a whole other league, one that even the Fresh Prince couldn't comprehend.

It was time to make the big leap, he knew. "The Fresh

Prince of Bel Air'' had served him well; it had been far more than a foot in the door. But the time had come to say goodbye and move ahead. There was one season remaining on his contract, and he made it clear that he wasn't going to re-sign, that this would be the end.

He was putting all his eggs in one basket, but it turned out to be a basket of huge proportions. *Independence Day* not only tapped into a zeitgeist of UFOs and the truth being out there, it was also one of the most perfect popcorn space movies since *Star Wars*.

Its pull on audiences seemed almost magnetic. On its opening weekend—which, just as it should have been, was the July 4 weekend, 1996—it opened on 2,400 screens and took in $83.5 million, a new record for that period.

But there was more to *Independence Day* than massive numbers. Although few people thought about it, then or even later, the film broke new ground—it offered a black hero saving the planet. We'd come a long, long way.

But one person who saw its significance straight away was Will Smith.

"I was happy to be a black man saving the world in *Independence Day*," he said. "Black people have been saving the world for years, only nobody knew it."

He went where no African-American had gone before, and came back a true star. At the age of twenty-eight he'd conquered virtually every field of entertainment.

However, he was still far too young to sit back and rest on his laurels. There was still plenty of work to be done, and he was in huge demand. Everybody wanted a piece of Will Smith. He'd become a new talisman of success—get him in your movie, and it would be a hit.

But he'd already signed on for his next project, with someone he simply couldn't turn down—Steven Spielberg. *Men In Black,* while ostensibly another dose of science fiction, essentially returned him to pure comedy—the thing he did so well and so naturally. And it proved to be *the* summer hit of 1997.

The film didn't just keep Will on top of the box-office

charts, but also brought him back to the music charts. With Jazzy Jeff, the Fresh Prince had recorded his last tracks in 1993, for their *Code Red* album, whose sales had been relatively meager. Now it was Will Smith who was rapping again, on the *Men in Black* theme song. Of course, it couldn't fail, and it didn't. It went all the way to number one on the *Billboard* Hot 100. And along the way, Will also signed a new recording contract with Columbia Records. Things had come full circle.

Will had become *the* breakthrough black actor. But the truth was, throughout his professional life, Will had been breaking through all the barriers of race. His music never had the anger or belligerence that characterized so much of hip-hop. What the Fresh Prince offered in his rap was entertainment, geared at a generation rather than a color. He offered universals, not specifics, and appealed every bit as much to whites as to blacks. There was nothing that threatened the power structure, nothing even to cause offense. It was put down by others in the genre as "suburban rap," but what the duo was doing was opening doors for others to follow, to make hip-hop the popular musical form of the nineties.

Much the same was true of his television series. It offered up an "edge" of sorts, but one that was largely blunted. It never tried to proclaim that it was from the street or the ghetto—places that had never been part of Will's past, either in fact or fiction. It was designed as primetime entertainment, nothing more or less, and that meant that its mission was to appeal to the largest possible number of people.

In the case of Will's films, that applies on an even greater scale, with the possible exception of *Where The Day Takes You,* which was at heart an American art film. A lot of money had been invested in each of the productions, and the aim was to make a profit. And more or less, they all have.

None of that makes Will Smith a sellout. What it does

make him is a star who can now command up to $12 million a movie, and has first choice on any number of scripts. Someone, in fact, who can do whatever he wants, whether it's make a record, play golf in the 150-yard hole at his house, or put his own money into Spike Lee's *Get On The Bus,* a film about the Million Man March—an event in which Will participated.

Mass popularity is always going to be derided by those who haven't achieved it, particularly if it's their ultimate goal. Those who criticize Will, who call him names and accuse him of this, that, and the other, are mostly those who don't have the talent to reach the pinnacle themselves. It's jealousy.

He's blazed a path for other African-American performers. Without a Jazzy Jeff and Fresh Prince, would an artist like Tupac Shakur have sold in the millions? Without "The Fresh Prince of Bel Air" would a comedy show like "Living Single" or "Brandy" have had a chance? And without Will breaking box office records in *Independence Day* would some younger black actor have a chance at a starring role?

He'd be the first to agree that luck has played a definite part in his rise. Being in the right place at just the right time has helped plenty of careers. But when you add luck to talent and ambition, you end up with a fairly unstoppable combination, one that can overcome almost any obstacle.

And Will's had his share of those to hurdle. For someone just over thirty, he's seen enough of the downs as well as the ups. Not that he's ever been forced to struggle, exactly, but at the end of the eighties, he received a letter telling him he owed the IRS well over a million dollars—money he simply didn't have. A house, cars, jewelry, clothes—those things he owned—but suddenly money was in very short supply. He was bankrupt in everything but name.

He was young, the money was pouring in as *He's the DJ, I'm The Rapper* went multi-platinum. It seemed like it would never stop. For the first time in his life Will was on his own, and he went wild—spend, spend, spend, everywhere he could.

The IRS letter was the warning that the pendulum had swung too far.

"There's nothing more sobering than having six cars and a mansion one day, and you can't even buy gas for the cars the next," he recalled.

As adversities go, it could have been worse. But the realization that he'd blown a fortune by the time he was twenty-one hit him hard, and left him more determined to make another, to succeed again.

He's also endured the pain of divorce, never an easy time, even for someone whose feet seem to be firmly on the floor. What naturally made it harder was the fact that the couple had a son, Willard Smith III, known, unsurprisingly, as Trey. From his birth it was apparent that Will absolutely doted on his son. Not to have him full-time had to be a devastating blow to him; instead of being a real parent he'd become another statistic, a weekend father. But in the aftermath, things have worked out surprisingly well, for Will, Trey, and Sheree Zampano, Will's ex.

Perhaps the biggest thing Will has going for him is his intelligence. It's all too easy to think that actors and musicians as a whole are a dumb breed, inarticulate, unable to see beyond their own egos. To a point, that's a valid view, but there'll always be exceptions, and Will Smith happens to be one of them. He could clown around in class and still take in his lessons, testing at a high college level. More than that, he could be erudite and perfectly charming (in fact, his teachers nicknamed him Prince Charming, for both his manner and his excuses—a nickname that would quickly be reduced to Prince, before Will himself added the Fresh).

A rapper needs to be smart and articulate—dropping rhymes is nowhere near as easy as it might seem; it takes a poet's ear for language and a very strong sense of rhythm and an actor who's being interviewed needs a strong command of words if he's not going to come across as stupid.

But to plan ahead, and also to learn from mistakes, that takes *real* brains. Will's applied a lot of thought to what he's done, to the moves he's made. It would have been easy, for example, for him to have ridden the success of "Fresh Prince of Bel Air" into a starring role in a not-so-hot movie, and in the short term that would have seemed like success. But Will had the ability to plan, to weigh his own limitations. He knew that in his first couple of seasons in television his acting was barely acceptable, and that it wasn't enough to carry a film. And so he started out with a tiny role in *Where The Day Takes You* and moved gradually from there. By the time he was ready to graduate to playing a central character on celluloid, he understood that to be taken seriously as a film actor he had to be cast against type, which led to *Six Degrees of Separation*.

His decision to abandon music in 1993 was reasoned. His most recent record—*Code Red,* his last collaboration with Jazzy Jeff—hadn't performed too spectacularly, selling only 300,000 copies, one-tenth of the amount their second album sold. But that wasn't really among his motivations for stopping. He needed to focus, to give his all to one thing, and acting was what was really filling his life. And hip-hop was moving in directions that he knew he couldn't try and emulate. By 1997, when he returned, all that had changed, of course. Hip-hop had taken a very poppish turn, largely thanks to the huge success of Puff Daddy. The time was ripe, not for the return of the Fresh Prince, but for Will Smith to hit the charts again.

And though success has piled on success, Will has managed to remain very grounded, very real. In some ways his early fame served him well—he was able to flush the extravagance out of his system, to understand how he'd been so stupid, and never do it again. By the time he was twenty-one, he could have been financially set up for life. Instead he was broke. Nine years later, he *is* set up for life. All the hype that's gone on, the words of praise—he's learned to take them with a grain of salt. He's realized that L.A., films, and television, is only the entertainment business, only a paycheck (however much it increases with each project); it's not real life. It's one of the reasons he doesn't make his home there, but a full hour's drive to the north, away from the hustle and bustle, where things take on different hues and a slower pace.

He's a person whom America has taken not only as one of its idols, but also to its heart. Between his music, his series, and his films, the country has had the opportunity to watch and hear his growth, to get to know him—after all, he's spent the last twelve years living his life in the public eye. We feel that we know him, and above all, we like him.

There's an openness about Will Smith. He comes across in a completely disingenuous manner that makes people feel that the line between the person and the characters he's played is very thin; that they are, in essence, him. His charm (which certainly hasn't deserted him since childhood) and easy humor aren't faked; he remains the goofball he was growing up in Philadelphia, albeit one who now knows when it's time to get down to business. The smile is real, the eyes shine with laughter and intelligence. He seems to take a real joy in what he does. He knows it's not "art" in the highest terms, and he doesn't try to make it something pretentious. It's entertainment, what's he's always tried to do, whether in a classroom for his friends, on a record, on TV, or on the big screen. He doesn't need to be Richard Wright to get his point across.

Inevitably, as a black man in America, he's seen a good deal of the prejudice that exists in this country. He's been stopped by the police for driving an expensive car, and had his right to a first-class seat in an airplane questioned. Being a star, in a privileged, insulated position, isn't enough to keep all the realities of everyday life at bay.

It could have altered his attitude and made him bitter; instead, he's realized that it's a view held by a racist minority who have still to wake up to the twentieth century.

Living well has been his best revenge, to become more popular with each year and each film.

"I'm comfortable with my life," he said. "I just try to put out good energy and it comes back tenfold. If there's one thing I've learned, it's that good begets good."

And in his case, it's begotten very good.

But there might be another explanation, one that's simpler, but which penetrates to the very heart of the American national psyche.

"It's the ears," Will suggested. "Americans have an ear fetish. Americans love people with big ears—Mickey Mouse, Goofy, and me."

Possible? Who knows? Jokes have a habit of containing a kernel of truth. But whatever the answer, the fact remains beyond dispute—Will Smith is a megastar.

CHAPTER ONE

NINETEEN-SIXTY-EIGHT was a pivotal year for race relations in America. The previous couple of years had seen tensions mount into riots at various points across the country—Watts in 1965, Detroit in '67. The Civil Rights Act might have become legislation, but words didn't seem to have made much difference in the way blacks were treated across the U.S.

The Black Panthers, feared or revered depending on your viewpoint and color, organized themselves to help the ghetto communities in whatever ways they felt necessary, and 1968 showed them to be strong and fearless. And down in Mexico City, black American athletes gave the raised fist Panther salute while being awarded their medals. Politics had entered sport in a controversial way.

The war in Vietnam raged more strongly than ever, even as peace marchers demonstrated against it. The first flowering of the hippie culture might have died, but its legacy was influencing a generation across the Western hemisphere. Caught between hatred and war and love and peace, the world was becoming a far more complex place in which to live than it had been just a decade before.

Some, though, just got on with their lives, doing what they could, concentrating on work and family, letting much of what was going on in the outside world pass them by. Willard Smith and his wife Caroline were like that. They were hardly blind to what was going on—they couldn't ignore it, since it was all over the newspapers and television—but they had other things on their minds in 1968.

Philadelphia was one of those cities whose inner city seemed like a powder keg waiting to blow at the time—it was volatile and occasionally violent. But in the Winfield neighborhood in the southwest of the city where the Smiths lived, things were calmer. It was made up of middle-class black families who still had to get up for work every day. The row houses were kept neat. These were people who'd managed to make something of themselves, and were proud of it. They didn't want a revolution, just a paycheck.

Willard Smith owned his own company, Arcac, which designed and installed commercial refrigeration equipment. Caroline worked at the Board of Education as an administrator. They had one daughter, Pamela, but now they were expecting another child.

When Caroline gave birth to a healthy boy on September 25, it was a major event in the family. This was the first son, someone to carry on the name. And so he became Willard C. Smith, Jr.

Three years later Pamela and Will would be joined by twins, Harry and Ellen, completing the Smith clan. It was quite a brood to pack into a row house, but the Smiths liked their neighborhood; they had friends there, it was home.

From the beginning, young Will was quite precocious. Unusually, as Caroline Smith remembered, "He could talk before he could walk," and once he'd found his voice there was no shutting him up. Each night his parents would read to him, and the Dr. Seuss books became a firm favorite at bedtime, with their nonsense and clever rhymes. They might even have had a subconscious influence on what he'd end up doing as a teenager, as Will noted many years later.

"If you listen to them a certain way, books like *Green Eggs and Ham* and *Hop On Pop* sound a lot like hip-hop."

Certainly Will was adept with language from a very young age. But he also showed an quick sense of humor, something that every member of the Smith family seemed to have.

"I was blessed with a really, really funny family," Will said. "Dinnertime was like a nightly laugh riot."

The humor could be verbal, or any of the antics young boys in particular seemed to find hilarious.

"Will did the gross things kids do, like put straws up his nose," younger sister Ellen remembered.

The Smiths were secure in their world. The parents worked hard every day, always giving their best, and that was the ethic that they strove to pass on to their children. You could have fun, but this was a life where you had to work, to love God and the church.

To Willard Smith, part of loving his kids was discipline. He had a very strong moral sense, and felt his offspring needed firm boundaries, limits on their behavior, and to immediately recognize the difference between right and wrong. And if they went beyond them, they knew what to expect. Caroline might be a softer touch, but with their father there was no chance of getting away unscathed.

"My father was the man with all the answers, the disciplinarian," Will told *TV Guide*. "He did his shaping by taking little chunks out of your behind."

But even when he was being spanked, Will wasn't about to let his humor vanish into tears.

"Will was punished first because he's older," said Harry. "Then he'd go around a corner and make faces so we'd laugh—and we'd get punished worse."

Hands might have hit backsides from time to time, and Will Sr. might have been tough on his son, but it was all done with love. And in return Will Jr. gained an incredible amount of respect for his parents.

"There are individual personality traits of celebrities and sports stars and people I admire," he revealed years later as an adult, "but the only people I ever idolized are my parents."

His maternal grandmother, Helen Bright, was also an important figure in his young life. She was active in her church, the Resurrection Baptist. She was "the woman . . . who put together the Easter egg hunt and the plays and the programs for the holidays" and made sure the Smith children were "in all her little plays."

Church on Sunday was a part of growing up, accepted without question. From an early age the idea of God was in Will's mind. But, as with most children, it remained fairly abstract until the family took what was really the vacation of a lifetime, an automobile trip across the United States.

"When I was about seven, we drove cross-country and saw Yellowstone and Mount Rushmore and the Alamo and the Grand Canyon. You see something beautiful, bigger than you, it mellows you, changes your attitude for life."

It was an experience that couldn't help but stay with him, one that truly brought home the idea of something much bigger and grander than himself. Fourteen years later, when some of his friends were coming out to L.A. to visit, Will (then beginning his tenure as star of " The Fresh Prince of Bel Air" insisted they drive across the continent to understand things in the same way he had.

Although Caroline Smith worked for the Board of Education, she wanted something better than a standard public school education for her own family. While it wasn't the easiest thing to afford with four kids, she insisted on them going to Catholic schools, where the grounding in essential subjects would be much better.

From kindergarten until eighth grade, Will went to Our Lady of Lourdes. He proved to be an adept student, shining in math, science, and English, where his writing—particularly of poetry—received high praise, which encouraged him to keep doing it.

But there was another side to Will at school. The sense of humor he displayed with his family at mealtimes couldn't help but peek through in the classroom, where the other kids proved to be a wonderful, captive audience.

It made him, as he rapidly discovered and enjoyed, the center of attention.

"It's always been fun for me to tell a story and make people laugh," he explained in *Cosmopolitan*. "I've always been a show-off, and uncomfortable when people weren't looking at me."

Looking at him was something the others couldn't help,

since, by his own admission, Will had a slightly odd appearance.

"When I was little, everybody always told me I looked like Alfred E. Neuman, the weird guy on the cover of *Mad Magazine*. I always had the square-looking fade hairdo, and I liked it, even though it made my ears stick out. One guy once told me I looked like a car with the doors open."

But being the clown took away from his looks. Having the joke, the story, the right line meant he was going to be accepted for his words and his humor, rather than victimized because he looked odd.

At home, though, he knew exactly where to draw the line, and there wasn't anyone—schoolmate, friend, anyone—who could get him to go past it.

"Even with peer pressure, there wasn't a friend I had who could pressure me to do something I knew would get me in trouble with my father. My father had so much control over me growing up—I didn't have too much of an opportunity to do things the wrong way. My father was always in my business. He always knew everything I was doing!"

One thing the whole family was involved with was music. Caroline was a good pianist, and there was a piano in the house. Will, with a strong ear, soon began to pick up bits and pieces, and it wasn't too long before his mother began teaching him the basics. But it was the drums, and rhythm, that really fascinated him. A set in the basement gave him the opportunity to learn, and much to the consternation of everybody else, he started to teach himself.

More than anything else a person can play, the drums require the coordination of all four limbs—no easy task, particularly for a young boy. But Will managed it. While he was never in the professional class, he could sit down at a drum kit and not seem like an idiot banging around.

All the kids were encouraged to play, and the family even formed a small ensemble, playing jazz for their own amusement. It was a regular part of family life, as Will noted.

"There were instruments around the house, and I just played a little of everything."

While he showed some talent, he didn't seem to have the motivation to really practice on any one thing. To him, messing around like this was just something the Smiths did; he never saw himself as a musician. When he was ten, Will Sr. bought him his own stereo, and he could begin listening to the funk that was the burgeoning black music scene in 1978.

The Smiths were a very close-knit family. It was all for one and one for all, well-illustrated by something that happened when Will was nine years old.

". . . My older sister (Pamela) must have been about fifteen. Some guys pulled a knife on me and took my money when I was coming home from school. I came in crying and my sister asked me why. I told her and she right away grabbed a baseball bat. We walked around for four hours looking for these guys. She had no concern for her own safety. Somebody had done something to her brother and she was going to do everything in her power to make sure they never did it again."

They never did find the thieves, but in some ways it didn't matter; this was a family with a great deal of love for each other.

Of course, there were plenty of things about which Will Sr. and Caroline needed to educate their children, and drugs, a problem which had barely existed when they were young, was one of them. But his father gave Will Jr. a graphic lesson about them that made a deep enough impact to last until the present day.

He put his son in the car and drove him through Philadelphia's skid-row area, a place the boy had been warned away from.

"He pointed to the bums sleeping in the doorways and said: 'This is what people look like when they do drugs.' "

It was all Will ever needed to hear.

*   *   *

In 1979, barely twelve years old, Will Smith underwent a life-changing experience. He was listening to the radio one day and a song came on by a band called Sugar Hill Gang. It was called "Rapper's Delight" and it was unlike anything that had entered his suburban Philadelphia world before. It had a beat as huge and funky as the music he loved, but over the top people were talking, rhyming, being funny.

It had never occured to him that you could talk over the top of music, let alone do it this way, with humor. Immediately he was lost to the whole idea.

It was rap, of course, and "Rapper's Delight" was the first record in the style to make any kind of commercial impact; indeed, it made a *huge* commercial impact, not only in the black market, but all across the board. To many it seemed like a novelty—the extended version ran some fifteen minutes, unheard-of at the time—but to others it was a clarion call.

Rap, in the days before it became known as hip-hop, was still a young form—street music, served up at parties and clubs in the Bronx, Brooklyn, and even in Manhattan. It was music that had taken its inspiration both from the "toasters" of Jamaican music (who were, by and large, the first rappers), and those who'd learned it was possible to take existing records, mess around with them on the turntables, and create a sound that was completely new. In New York it had been going on for a few years, slowly developing, with people like Kool Herc, Afrika Bambaataa, and Grandmaster Flash leading the way by playing the music and starting breakdance "crews." But it had remained quite underground, mostly a ghetto music, until Sylvia Robinson, who ran Sugar Hill Records in New Jersey, heard a bootleg tape of some live rap, and saw its commercial potential.

The Sugar Hill Gang was made up of three rappers, Big Bank Hank, Wonder Mike, and Master Gee, all trying out outdo and outboast each other as they took turns at the mic. The background took what had been a huge hit for Chic, "Good Times"—a song familiar to so many listeners— and used it as a bedrock for the words.

The refrain in the lyrics helped popularize the term hip-hop (supposedly created by Bronx rapper Starski the Love-bug). It wasn't even really representative of what was truly happening in the music, according to Grandmaster Caz.

"It didn't represent what MCing was, what rap and hip-hop was. It didn't represent what it truly was, but mainstream and nationally, it was everyone's first taste of what hip-hop was."

It hadn't even been the first rap record (that credit went to the Fatback Band), but with selling two million copies worldwide, and being played endlessly on urban radio, it might as well have been. For Will Smith in Philadelphia, it was his first taste. And he was immediately smitten.

"I started rapping as soon as I heard that first song. I rapped all day long until I thought my mom was going to lose her mind! Music, after all, has always been in my heart. At first, I did it as a hobby and I enjoyed it and got really good at it. When you enjoy what you do, you're going to get really good at it. And I just concentrated on it."

For Will, it offered the perfect combination. In school, he was good at English, at using words, and he'd been writing poetry. He could crack the class up with his humor, and he loved being the center of attention. Nothing brought all that together like being a rapper. And suddenly, particularly among black youth, rap was the music of choice.

As Jeff Townes, who in a few years would become better known as DJ Jazzy Jeff, Will's musical partner, explained,

"When rap came out, there was this buzz: *This* is something new. We never heard this before, but somebody made this especially for us. This is *our* music because our parents don't like it, our grandmothers don't like it. But *we* like it."

In the wake of "Rapper's Delight," hip-hop was everywhere. Overnight a whole string of records started to come out, some good, some bad, and some that took the art form further. In the hands of the Sugar Hill Gang it had been party music, and that would remain one strand, but it quickly began to take on more serious overtones. But in all its forms, hip-hop was nothing less than a musical and social revolution for African-Americans. Within a year it was everywhere. All the kids, the teenagers, wanted to be a part of it.

"When you grow up in any urban area, particularly a black area, you can't escape it," Will explained. "Rap is the urban music. Everybody in the street is a rapper, or a DJ, or a beat box. Hip-hop is a culture. It's not just music, it's a way of life."

Even in Winfield, far removed from the ghetto, that was the case. But being smart, articulate, and funny, Will had a head start over many potential rappers. And it didn't take long before he was composing his own raps.

Initially, though, he wanted to be a DJ, the person behind the "wheels of steel" (turntables) who contributed the music to the art, scratching a beat on the discs, and putting together the snatches of other records that made the beat and backbone for something new.

And that was what he did for a while, at the block parties that were an integral part of hip-hop's early development all over the country. It was a free-for-all, a mass competition where people would challenge each other and show their skills.

But there were plenty who were better than him, even as he realized his talents might lie more with his words than cutting up the music and scratching the beat. Once he started rapping in public there was no stopping him.

"My reputation came from beating other rappers in street challenges. I never lost a street battle."

It was a time when every kid who could drop a rhyme was able to dream of being a star, of being known, and Will was no exception. At the same time, he knew he could do almost anything. He was bright, happy, well-adjusted, and he felt secure surrounded by a family with plenty of love.

But something was about to happen that would turn his world upside down.

In 1981, when Will was thirteen, his parents gathered the children together. They had an announcement to make—they were getting divorced.

It was a bombshell. Will Sr. and Caroline had been very careful to hide their own problems from the kids, but the fact was that they couldn't live together as a couple any more. For Will, Harry, and Ellen (Pamela was nineteen, and in college, so a little more removed from the situation) it seemed almost unbelievable. The arrangements had been made. Will and the twins would continue to live with their mother, and they would see their father often—just because he wouldn't be living there didn't mean that he wouldn't take a great deal of interest in their upbringing.

One thing that was stressed to the children was that the split had nothing to do with them, or that it would alter any of their parents' feelings for them.

"We never felt like our parents didn't love us," Will said. "No matter how difficult things got or how angry someone may have gotten, no matter what happened in our lives, we always felt that we had somewhere to go. You can't spring off into the world from a flimsy base. You've got to have a solid base to jump from."

And both Will Sr. and Caroline were determined to give their offspring that. They only difference was that they'd be doing it individually, instead of together.

That proved to be exactly the way it happened. Although his father wasn't around every night, Will still saw him frequently, and the weight of paternal discipline didn't prove to be any less. Will Sr. was intent on molding his son to be an upright, moral man.

The following year Will graduated from eighth grade, and Our Lady of Lourdes school. The next step was Overbrook High School. He was going from being a big fish in a small pond to a minnow in an ocean, but he had two things going for him—his ability to be class clown and his growing reputation as a rapper.

He'd even put together a duo with a friend, Clarence "Cate" Holmes, who quickly became known as Ready Rock-C. He was the human beat box, who could get rhythmic sounds out of any part of his body—the kind of person who was a member of all rap crews at the time before drum machines became commonplace.

Will had been writing and honing his raps, winning street contests, and now he had Ready Rock-C working with him, he felt it was time to move things up a notch. Although he was only fourteen, the big time was beckoning in the distance. The duo contacted Word Up, a local record label that was specializing in rap, run by Dana Goodman, who also happened to be the label's producer.

Goodman listened to what was on offer to see if Will could deliver the goods. He had the quality—what was missing was the quantity; there simply wasn't enough material. Goodman advised that they "go home and get more material" then come back and see him. The door for the future was left open, and that was enough for Will.

He was energized about a possible rap career—Goodman hadn't said no, after all—but he had other responsibilities to consider. And the main one was school.

Will might have shone at Our Lady of Lourdes, but Overbrook High was a completely different place. He was surrounded by kids who didn't know him and who all had to prove themselves. Will decided that the best thing was to carry on where he had left off, and establish his reputation as class clown all over again.

While most class clowns tended to be kids who used humor to cover for a lack of book smarts, Will was the exception.

"I'd cut up in class, but still take in what the teacher was saying."

That was proved by the fact that he kept up his good grades in math and sciences, while becoming virtually top in his year in English. He even played in the high school band for a while. He was, essentially, a good kid, but "I was just silly all the time. People I went to school with probably remember me as a jackass.''

Jackass he might have been, but he was one with a silver tongue. He could turn on the charm, the smile, the gift of the humorous gab and talk his way out of anything.

''I always used to get into silly trouble, but I was always so charming, I could smooth talk my way out of any situation.''

He was the kid with the creative excuses, the ones so preposterous and funny that the teachers just had to accept them. It wasn't long before the teachers in the faculty lounge came up with their own name for Will Smith— Prince Charming.

His grades were above average, but Will wasn't really applying himself to the work.

''I got the grades mainly to please my parents,'' he explained. ''I didn't think I'd ever use what I learned. But in my rap and as an actor, it's amazing how much of what I did learn comes back to me. It all pays off in the end. I just didn't know it back then.''

His father had always told Will that he needed to focus, and it was a lesson he'd taken to heart from an early age. What he was focusing on, though, wasn't schoolwork, but rapping.

The whole rap scene in Philly was developing at a remarkable pace, and Will was becoming quite involved in it. Apart from records, it still revolved around parties, and he was taking part in those, too. With the reputation he'd acquired, he began charging for his services.

''When I was sixteen and everybody else was going to parties and having fun, I said, 'Okay, if I'm going to a party, I might as well get paid for it.' ''

It was a natural extension of the work ethic his father had instilled in Will. When he was fifteen, Will Sr. had given him and Harry a project for the summer—they had to tear down and rebuild a brick wall at the house. At first it didn't seem too daunting, but as they got to work, it dragged on forever. The summer vacation passed and they were nowhere near done. They worked on it after school and on weekends, "one brick at a time," doing everything, even the cement mixing, themselves. When it was finally complete, months later, they could look at their work with pride.

"Dad told me and my brother, 'Now don't you all ever tell me you can't do something.' "

Like most growing teenage boys, Will was interested in girls. There, too, he was precocious. Other boys were bragging about their experience, and Will didn't want to be left behind. But he found, when it came to the real thing, it was a case of running before he could walk.

"It was with my girlfriend in eighth grade . . . Anyway, it happened at my house and all, but it took me, like, thirty minutes to figure out how to get the rubber to work—sorry, Mom, the *prophylactic*. I just didn't know how to work it. It was dark, too, and I dropped it and then I had to turn the lights on to find it. Anyway, finally it really didn't . . . um . . . happen, because I got a little ahead of myself. So to speak."

By the time Will was sixteen, his time seemed to be divided between school and rapping. He'd found a way of putting words across that was funny as well as skillful—a way that was just Will.

"I had a pretty new style that everyone was finding interesting. I can make people laugh on a party scene. . . . It was a hobby and it just took off."

Things were going along, and Will had hopes of making a record, doing something in rap, but he never imagined it as a real career. Even though others were doing well, it wasn't something he could visualize for himself. After all, you made money by working, and music just didn't seem like work.

"I thought I'd end up with some nice little nine-to-five job someday," he admitted in *Cinescape*.

But in 1986, something happened that would change all that, a meeting with someone else who'd been making a name for himself in the growing Philadelphia rap scene.

Jeff Townes was a DJ. He'd grown up not too far from Will. Neither of them were "street" kids, by any stretch of the imagination; in fact, being middle-class and suburban, they really countered the stereotypical image of blacks that most white Americans had.

Just like Will, he'd been smitten with rap from the first time he heard it. But for Jeff, it wasn't so much the words as the music that attracted him, the way a DJ could manipulate the sounds that already existed on vinyl to create something different and new. He started DJing when he was ten.

"I used to call myself a bathroom DJ," he said, "because I would tag along to parties with older DJs and finally get my chance to go on when they went to the bathroom!"

It was a small beginning, but one he made effective use of. Whereas most people were cutting up George Clinton and James Brown, and taking their beat by sampling "Funky Drummer," Jeff's heart was elsewhere. His parents always had plenty of jazz albums around the house, and that was not only the music he'd grown up on, but also the music he loved. And Jeff saw no reason why that couldn't be a part of hip-hop. It swung, it could be funky and melodic. He began to use it when he had his turn at the wheels of steel, and it immediately set him apart from all the other DJs plying their trade, earning him his nickname, DJ "Jazzy" Jeff.

At the same time, the price of home recording equipment, primarily portable four-track recorders, began to plummet. Jeff bought one, and set up a small studio in his parents' basement, where he could experiment and perfect the ideas he had.

When he appeared on a local rap radio show in Philly, he created something of a sensation. He used what he'd learned in the basement to transform material beyond all recognition, with all manner of new techniques. Suddenly Jazzy Jeff was a big deal around town.

He put his own crew together, and kept playing all over Philadelphia, making some money, and making a name for himself. There were dreams of making it big, but for that he needed the right rapper, and Jeff hadn't managed to find him. Yet.

Early in 1986, Jeff and his crew had agreed to play a party, which was on Will's block.

"I was the best DJ in Philadelphia," Jeff told *Disney Adventures*, "and I had heard of Will, but I already had someone I worked with. But when I played that party on Will's block, naturally he was there. He asked if he could rap for a while and I said yes. He started rapping and I started cutting, and it was like natural chemistry. He flowed with what I did and I flowed exactly with what he did and we knew it. We just clicked the whole night long. The chemistry between us was so good. I went home and dreamed about him. I got his number and we got together."

They began to work in Jeff's basement, putting tracks together. Things were going well, but it didn't really take off until a few weeks later.

"I bought this canned fart spray and sprayed it at a party," Jeff recalled. "We just cracked up. When I found Will was down with the same humor, that was when we really clicked."

They began writing and recording in earnest. But there was a fly in the musicial ointment—school. Prince Charming had been getting reasonable grades, and getting by, but then one of Will's teachers told Caroline that he "was testing at a college level but just barely passing."

Caroline gave her son an ultimatum, which Will Sr. backed up. It was time for him to get serious about school. Rap might be fine for his free weekends, but he needed to focus on academics. And if he didn't, he'd pay the price. Which did happen one day. Will Sr. had told his oldest son he'd need help with a job one morning. It was going to be tricky, and he wanted Will bright and fresh at 6 A.M. to begin. Will had been working at a party and arrived home just fifteen minutes before he was supposed to be up.

Inevitably the worst happened. The job was at a deli, working with electricity in a flooded basement. Will, who was supposed to hold the flashlight so his father could see what he was doing, began to doze. The beam wavered, the light fell into the water, and suddenly there was a high scream.

"My father sounded like Patti LaBelle."

When Will managed to find the flashlight and get it working again, he saw his father, hair standing on end, fingertips smoking, and decidedly unhappy. Will Sr. brought his arm back and punched his son on the chest so hard that he was able to feel it, he said, every day for the next ten years.

It was a good object lesson in priorities—and his dad's punch. He agreed to get serious about school.

He did, and by the time he sat his SAT exams, he performed extremely well. He applied to colleges around the country, and was immediately accepted at Milwaukee School of Engineering. There was even talk of him going to Massachussets Institute of Technology (the prestigious MIT).

"I was talking to the guys from MIT, and there was some kind of two-year pre-engineering prep course that they were interested in having me apply for."

But he never did. Focus as he might on improving his test scores, Will's heart was in the music he was making in his spare time. He and Jeff had recruited Will's partner, Ready Rock-C, to help fill out their crew. The writing developed quickly. Jeff would provide the music, and Will the raps.

"We'd sit down and talk about things first," Will explained. "The songs come from our own experience."

And that experience had little to do with ghetto life and hardship. Instead they found themselves addressing the universal issues of growing up. Video games and monster movies, girls. It was black music, yes, but there was also plenty in there that white kids could relate to.

While Jeff already had his nickname, somehow a rapper called Prince Charming didn't sound too good. Considering it, Will decided to keep the Prince and add something from hip-hop language—Fresh.

"At the time the word Fresh was *the* word. It was street talk for cool, the best."

And so DJ Jazzy Jeff and the Fresh Prince were born.

It didn't take long for them to put together a tape of material and take it down to Dana Goodman at Word Up, the producer who'd encouraged Will to come back when he had more material.

The result was instantaneous. In his senior year of high school, Will Smith had a recording contract. A few weeks later, the first single by DJ Jazzy Jeff and the Fresh Prince hit the streets. It was called "Girls Ain't Nothing But Trouble."

It took off as a teen anthem, not just in Philly, but all over the country. Boys could understand the way girls were viewed, and girls—even if they didn't agree with it—could see the point. This wasn't the hard sound of Public Enemy, preaching a new political gospel. This was pop music, pure and simple. It was made by teens and aimed at teens—the people who were the biggest record-buying market. And from the beginning, that was the market with which it resonated.

Not that there wasn't a backlash. A few journalists, in the forefront of politcial correctness, called the song sexist.

"That's a ridiculous, idiotic opinion," Will responded. "The rap is a personal story, told with a sense of humor, rather than a statement of general attitude."

And even some members of the hip-hop community criticized them for making a record that was so lightweight, when they should have been making music that was more black or more vital. They couldn't win.

Or could they?

Virtually before they knew what was happening, the duo had a hit single. And not only in America, but also England, where it rocketed into the charts. With one disc they'd gone from being nobodies to international stars, selling 100,000 copies of "Girls Ain't Nothing But Trouble" along the way. It wasn't a bad debut, and even more remarkable considering Will was still only a senior in high school.

The sudden success forced him to look at what was going on in his life. He'd been rapping for years, and never giving it a great deal of thought as a way to make real money. Now that door was open for him.

On the other hand, his parents wanted him to go on to college, to get a real education that would set him up for the rest of his life.

Should he follow his heart, or take the path his parents wanted? It was a hard decision. People were clamoring for Jazzy Jeff and the Fresh Prince to make an album and to appear live. There was talk of major tours.

With one hit single under their belt, and plenty more songs on tape, Will and Jeff felt they were ready to take the next step and make an entire album.

There were offers coming in from other record companies, and some big numbers were bandied around. And it was apparent to the duo that they'd need to move to a larger label if they were going to have the kind of impact they felt was possible. Word Up simply didn't have the ability to do what was needed to market a record and make them into the stars they hoped they could be.

Naturally, Dana Goodman didn't want to let them go, and when Will and Jeff finally signed with Jive records, who'd had plenty of success during the 1980s with bands such as Whodini, he wasn't too happy.

The relationship with Jive was a lot calmer. Early in 1987 DJ Jazzy Jeff and the Fresh Prince released their first album, *Rock the House*. Its title track was penned by "extra special associate member" Ready Rock-C, who was still being billed as "the human beat box."

It was a strong record that took up where "Girls Ain't Nothing But Trouble" left off. It didn't pretend to be hard or savvy. It was nothing more than a pair of suburban black teens relating their experiences in a way that everybody their age—regardless of race, creed, or color—could understand. Inevitably there were the boasts that characterized all hip-hop, claiming to be the best ever, but that was par for the course. Musically it continued the light groove they'd already begun to mine, building from Jeff's collection of jazz records.

"I really love jazz," he explained to *Rolling Stone*. "It freaks people out when they ask me who I listen to and I name six artists that basically a lot of people haven't heard of."

But that, along with Will's humorous, everyday teenage raps, was what set them apart. When everybody else was trying to be as funky as possible, digging through the James Brown songbook for a beat, and the old Parliament/Funkadelic catalogue for a bassline, Jeff had a fresh field to plunder. By its very nature, the music swung, and it was, in every sense of the word, fresh.

With better distribution and promotion, *Rock the House* found an even larger audience than the first single, selling some 600,000 copies. It was a remarkable debut for a pair of teens, one of whom was still a high school senior, and it earned them their first gold record (a gold record equates to sales of 500,000 copies).

At that point, Will knew what he had to do. He sat down with his mother, and told her he wanted to become a rapper, to put the idea of college on hold.

Then he had to face his father, "who was also none too thrilled with the course of events. Still, my father basically said, 'Okay. Take a year. If it works, God bless you. If it doesn't, you'll go to college.' "

Even though the decision had been made, Caroline Smith held out hope.

"My mother told all the schools I got into to hold the dorm room, just hoping I'd change my mind. I didn't."

Will was seventeen years old, with a major hit single and a gold album. As far as he was concerned, the sky was the limit.

CHAPTER TWO

ALTHOUGH the duo had honed their work in front of party audiences in Philadelphia, they didn't tour to back up *Rock the House*. The offers were there, but they chose instead to throw themselves straight into making a follow-up, to really capitalize on the audience they'd created for their music.

Another factor might have been the violence that seemed to accompany hip-hop tours around America. It could be ugly, with plenty of fights, and more than a few shootings—hardly the right backdrop for people who made such lighthearted sounds.

And who would they have toured with? None of the other people in the scene were making music like theirs. Hard-hitting seemed to be the order of that day, and that hardly described DJ Jazzy Jeff and the Fresh Prince. Theirs wasn't the anger of the ghetto, but the tinkle of a sprinkler on a suburban lawn, an hour's drive and a whole lifestyle away.

The first flush of success didn't change either Will or Jeff. They had money now, more than they'd dreamed of, but they were still living at home, working on something they loved—to the extent that it seemed to take up all their time. With his mother around, and his father not far away, there wasn't much chance for Will to get flashy or develop a big head.

Not that he wanted to; both he and Jeff were completely focused on the new music they were creating. *Rock The House* had given them a foundation, and now they wanted to create a structure, something that was completely different from anything else that was going on in hip-hop.

The remarkable thing was that they succeeded. Given a completely free hand by their label, they came up with *He's the DJ, I'm the Rapper,* the first hip-hop double album. It was a huge amount of material, all of which went past the sounds they'd created before. Jeff had really refined his techniques, creating layers behind Will's voice.

And Will, too, had come a long way. He was still the same person he'd always been, but the rhymes had been worked on solidly, smoothed out, revised again and again into something that complemented the music. It was different, it had pop appeal, but it was very much still black music—it couldn't be anything else.

"Our music is black music," Will asserted in *Rolling Stone.* "Our families are black; we come from black backgrounds. When I was writing "Parents Just Don't Understand," I wanted my friends to be able to relate to it. People have to label things. To each individual it's something different.

"People listen to our music, but they never really listen. People don't see the sarcasm. We try to sneak messages in, because people don't want to be preached to."

"Parents Just Don't Understand" was the album's breakout track. Released as a single, it caught the imagination of a nation's youth even more than "Girls Ain't Nothing But Trouble," helped along by a humorous video that was quickly in heavy rotation on MTV. And what kid couldn't tell a story of shopping for clothes with his or her mother?

"In 'Parents Just Don't Understand,' we wanted to write about something everybody could relate to. I wasn't trying to appeal to a white audience, or do anything different. I was writing about what I related to, what I thought was interesting. It's from my own experience."

But it was far from the only piece on the album with teen appeal. "Nightmare on My Street" (which became the next single) paid homage to horror movies. Both cracked the Billboard Top Twenty, and spurred along sales of the album, which would eventually go triple platinum. It was an incredible achievement for hip-hop, which was still seen as music of marginal interest.

In many ways, the duo fueled the hip-hop explosion. As had happened with the first single, the biggest group buying their records wasn't black youth. White kids found plenty of themselves in the words, and enough pop in the music for it to be readily acceptable. While they hadn't set out to do so, DJ Jazzy Jeff and the Fresh Prince had become one of rap's first big crossover acts. They weren't just successful, they were huge, and that, as it had done before, brought a backlash from the more "serious" acts, accusing them of being frivolous, irrelevant, or, even worse, suburban. Some even accused them of making music purely for white people.

True, it wasn't from the street—but not all black families live in ghettoes. There were plenty who enjoyed middle-class lives, like Will and Jeff. All the criticism, a good deal of which had come from rapper Big Daddy Kane, forced Will to reply.

"I don't think anyone can dictate what's black and what's not black," he said. "Big Daddy Kane is ignorant and doesn't realize what black really means. He thinks being articulate is being white. We're trying to show the world, and black kids, that you can dress nicely and still be considered black."

But they certainly weren't about to let themselves be restricted by color. Both Will and Jeff were individuals, expressing themselves. Whoever picked up on that was fine with them.

"We *are* humorous," Jeff pointed out, "we like to have fun. We let our personalities run through our work. Both of us have a good sense of humor and we don't act any differently when we make a record. You don't have to come on rough to rap. If there's funny stuff on our album, it comes from us."

Will agreed completely, and went even further.

"We make it universal. My point of view isn't limited. It's very broad. It's more than the black experience."

But he would have readily agreed that it didn't try to be the entire black experience. Will was writing about the things he knew. He was also insistent in doing it in a way that avoided cursing or profanity, and for a very good reason.

"I would never do anything that my mother couldn't turn on her radio and listen to," he said. "I would never do anything to offend my family."

It was a stance that set Jeff and Will apart from the majority of rappers, who seemed to find shock a major weapon in their arsenal. But it did fit in perfectly with their style of being themselves. With two hit singles and a record that was scurrying up the charts, it was easy to forget they were little more than kids, and good kids at that. They'd never been rebels, with or without a cause. If anything, what they reflected was something that had been quite ignored in music—the middle-class black experience. In doing that, they achieved more in unifying black and white than most hip-hop, which, on the surface at least, simply wanted to be divisive.

In the end, Will finally wondered, "Why do you have to compare DJ Jazzy Jeff and the Fresh Prince with other rappers? Rap is just like any other kind of music. You can't compare Luther Vandross to Michael Jackson, so why do we have to be compared to Public Enemy or Tone Loc? All rap is real."

In terms of sales, theirs was far more real than most. The album continued to sell worldwide. "Parents Just Don't Understand" took on almost classic status among kids, and its follow-up became another major hit.

DJ Jazzy Jeff and the Fresh Prince were the big stars they'd always hoped to be, even if they could never have imagined it in reality.

There was fame, and there was definitely fortune. Once the royalties from sales started to roll in, it wasn't in a trickle, but a torrent. And quite cannily, they added to the money by starting their own 900 line—a toll-line kids could call to hear daily updates from Will and Jeff about the record, their lives, and the tour that was about to begin. Since they were so hot, the calls were coming fast and furious (over two million in the first six months the line was operating), and they were making money hand over fist. It got to the point where executives at Jive Records had bets going about which would generate more income for the duo—royalties or the line.

It seemed like an idyllic life, making music and getting paid big money for doing it. But now they needed to get their show on the road, quite literally, opening for Run DMC, with whom they'd also performed on the pilot of "Yo! MTV Raps."

Will and Jeff were determined to do it in style; they wanted to give their audiences a night to remember, which meant plenty of action and plenty of people. The crew they assembled for the tour was large, with plenty of dancers, their own bodyguards, and far more roadies than they really needed, considering their only equipment was Jeff's set-up.

But these people were all friends, people who wanted to get out of Philly and hang with the stars. They were suddenly big men, with more friends than they could count. Since they lacked the maturity to separate friend from sycophant, Will and Jeff took them all.

The tour could have been a much wilder experience than it turned out to be. Away from home for the first time, with fans all over the world, and plenty of temptation in every form, Will and Jeff could have gone completely crazy. It was to their credit that they didn't. They were largely insulated from the day-to-day realities, but there were still a few home truths that registered, as Will recalled.

"You know, you get out to Albany, Georgia, and the promoter didn't make his money, so he doesn't want to pay you."

Both Jeff and Will called home regularly, both to keep in touch and to keep themselves grounded, and Will insisted that he was still the same person.

"Success hasn't changed me too much. Now the difference is I can get two hamburgers instead of one."

Every day they were out on the road was costing money. With their huge entourage they were spending far more than they could hope to take in. Will and Jeff insisted that it should all be done in style, that everyone should be livin' large.

Limousines, fancy restaurants, shopping. There were plenty of ways to show you had the cash. When the tour hit Atlanta, a call went out to the Gucci store there, instructing them to close their doors for a private shopping party. The crew spent several thousand dollars—all from Will and Jeff's pockets.

It was a movable party, and even when the tour was finished, it didn't stop. Back home Will continued to spend money like it was going out of fashion. He loved jewelry, and treated himself to a gold necklacke with "Fresh Prince" spelled out, the F and P in diamonds.

Then there was the house, a true mansion just outside Philly, in the plush suburb of Merion. As soon as he'd bought it, Will had the house redecorated in a way that could only be called "late adolescent." There was a basketball hoop in the living room, a pool room in the entryway (with frequent bets on the games), and a hot tub smack in the middle of the bedroom. The kitchen had rows of juice bottles and cold cuts—more like a convenience store than a place where someone might cook.

And when that didn't prove enough, Will took to buying cars. Six of them, including a Corvette, a Camaro, and a Suburban. If it caught his eye, Will bought it. And every vehicle, of course, had to be equipped with a massive stereo system.

It was livin' large indeed. Surrounded by admirers, Will thought he was king of the hill. But others had their doubts, including his parents. When Will boasted to his dad that he owned six cars, his father replied, "Why do you need six cars when you only have one butt?" which wasn't exactly what his son wanted to hear. And all the money and fame couldn't keep real life in America completely at bay. The police always wanted to know about young black males driving expensive cars.

"In the two years I had my Corvette, I probably got stopped thirty-five or forty times. At least five to ten of those times, I was told I was stopped because ' . . . we want to know where you got this car.' A young black guy with a nice car is going to get stopped, period. And the cops will tell you that."

For all the times he was made to feel like a criminal, there were many more that he felt like Croesus. He could afford to buy anything he wanted—and he did.

"Even if it was ugly, I bought it," he admitted. "Once I flew to London and Tokyo just to buy clothes."

He was flying high, and it looked like it would never stop. But even as he was doing it, he was wondering why all the riches, the possessions, and the power didn't leave him satisfied.

"I spent a long time trying to figure out how things could be going so well, and I could be so unhappy."

It all seemed like the most fun a person could have, but looking back later, he'd realize that "there was nothing funny about it. It was a matter of being young, wild, and stupid. But there was nothing anyone could have done. At that age, with that amount of money, it's difficult to handle. And because I was eighteen, the checks came to me. So it was difficult for anyone to intervene in the ludicrous behavior I was displaying. Besides, I didn't listen to anyone. Everything my parents taught me went right out the window as soon as that cash hit the bank account."

In truth, there was more money hitting that bank account than even Will, with his extravagant tastes, could spend. At twenty he was a millionaire. But he was trying his hardest to let it all slip through his fingers.

"One year I spent eight hundred thousand dollars," he admitted. "I went through it so fast, it made my head spin. Being able to buy anything you want makes you a little crazy."

It also made Will Sr. and Caroline very sad. They'd worked hard to bring their son up with proper values. Granted, he hadn't gone the way of many—he was still perfectly upright in his dealings, no drugs, and he hadn't become stupid with girls—but to watch him hemmorhaging money hurt them. For Will Sr. it went even further. He was a self-made man who worked every day to support his family. He was appalled at Will's behavior.

"He saw me blowing money that could allow me to set myself up for the rest of my life," Will said.

Not that everything was utter money madness. Even at the height of their fame from *He's The DJ, I'm The Rapper,* Will and Jeff knew they had to begin work on another record; they were hardly ignoring that. Instead of Philly, though, they decided that a more exotic location would be conducive to work. Somewhere like the sunny Bahamas, working at legendary Compass Point studios. They rented a house there (owned by singer Robert Palmer), and flew their crew down to help with inspiration.

The trip ended up lasting two weeks. What had been planned as flat-out work somehow got sidetracked by the sea and sand, and the presence of so many friends. They did manage to complete four tracks, but it quickly became apparent that this wasn't what they needed to get an album done.

If the duo needed any confirmation that they'd been the real crossover hip-hop act of 1988, it came at the start of January the following year. The truth was that they really *had* done more than any other hip-hop act to expose the music to a white audience, which would in turn help it become the biggest music of the nineties. But within the business, although it sold well, rap was seen as marginal, still very much black music for a black market. It was big, but not massive.

For their contribution to changing that, DJ Jazzy Jeff and the Fresh Prince found themselves at the American Music Awards, winning in the Best Rap Album and Best Rap

Artist categories—real recognition from the establishment. And, a month later, they received the first-ever Grammy for Best Rap Single, their award for the phenomenal success of "Parents Just Don't Understand."

It was the first year the Grammys had honored rap, deemed it worthy of an award, although the music had existed commercially for a decade. (It was also the first year they had a "Metal" category, and that music had been around for almost twenty years.) Unfortunately, although the establishment was finally willing to admit the music existed, they didn't seem to consider it on a par with their other awards. The Grammys for rap would be given out before the main body of the televised show, tossed in with all the technical awards, as if no one was really interested.

Naturally, neither Will nor Jeff was happy about that. They'd made music the equal of anyone else, and sold more records than many who'd be up onstage, making their speeches. To write off rap so blithely smacked heavily of racism. Invited to attend and pick up their award, they both declined.

"It's like going to school for twelve years and then not being able to walk across the stage," was their explanation, and although the people at the Grammys were angry at such a response, the point was taken. The following year the rap category became part of the main event. But by then, thanks in part to Will and Jeff, it could no longer be denied.

While neither of the two was political, they felt they'd had no choice. Their music wasn't second-class, and neither were they. Noticeably, however, the people who'd been so quick to criticize them for not cleaving to the black ideal of rap didn't spring to their defense when they did stand up.

Will and Jeff were rich beyond their wildest dreams, lauded and feted, hanging out in Los Angeles with celebrities like Eddie Murphy. The money they were making was passing through their hands like water. They were defining the whole idea of livin' large.

There was only one problem. All the checks coming their way—royalties for their records, income from the 900 line (which alone reportedly grossed $10 million)—were for the full amount. They were their own bosses; no taxes had been taken out along the way. Young, foolish, not bothering with such minor details as accountants and business managers, they assumed that everything they received was theirs.

But it wasn't. Of the three certainties in life—birth, death, and taxes—they'd forgotten the taxes.

The IRS, however, hadn't forgotten them, and one day, at his new home in Merion, Will received a letter from them. It was polite, calm, but stated quite clearly in black and white that he owed the government more than a million dollars that he'd somehow forgotten to pay.

Quite literally, overnight Will had gone from being a very rich young man to being broke. He was worse than broke, he was a debtor to the U.S. Government, owing more than he could really conceive of paying. In less than a year he'd gone from nobody to millionaire and back again.

"There's nothing more sobering than having six cars and a mansion one day and you can't even buy gas for the cars the next."

In short order he'd learned a very important lesson, but one that was going to prove very expensive. And he quickly learned another. All the hangers-on vanished out of his life as if he'd never existed, moving on to find the next party, the next sucker to want their company.

Will had to think. Not only about how he was ever going to pay off his huge tax bill, but also about the way he'd been living. He had to look hard at himself, ask some tough questions, and come up with some answers. He might be the Fresh Prince, but was the person the Fresh Prince had become really him?

Looking inside, he realized the answer had to be no.

That person, the one who'd gone crazy with his checkbook, was an abberation.

"I had a period in my life where I sought attention, had a little money, and wanted to flex it all. But the real person inside me eventually dictated how I had to act, how I had to behave, and how I had to treat people. My parents and my upbringing weighed out over the temptation of the glitter, the money, and all that. Who I am really wins every time."

Will had himself, he had his family, and he had his real friends. And he began to understand that that counted for a lot. It didn't come easily, but he sold his collection of cars, put the mansion on the market, and moved back in with his mother.

Finally he and Jeff were able to focus on their music again, even if there was a touch of desperation about it. Will needed the new album to be even bigger than the last one—that was his hope for paying off his taxes.

At the end of 1989, as the old decade closed, *And in this Corner* appeared. With everything riding on its success, Will hoped for the best. And hoped. And hoped.

There was no giant single this time, let alone two of them, and the disc didn't exactly fly out of the stores. In the two years since *He's the DJ, I'm the Rapper*, the whole climate of rap and the attitude towards it had changed. Will and Jeff had helped effect the breakthrough of hip-hop to the lucrative white market. Unfortunately, somewhere along the way they'd been left behind. They'd gone from the cutting edge to somewhere in the middle of the pack.

The album didn't flop, going past one million copies, sales were respectable enough to bring in some money. The single, "I Think I Can Beat Mike Tyson" was a hit in its own right and saw the duo nominated for their second Grammy. But it was quickly apparent that the Fresh Prince wasn't going to supply Will Smith with the million dollars he needed. He was going to have to look elsewhere.

"In 1990," Will said, "I was dealing with a decline in my music—at least in my eyes. I was looking for something new, something else to do."

What he didn't know was that a chance meeting was going to give him exactly that opportunity.

CHAPTER THREE

iT was all thanks to Disney, really. Will had flown out
to Los Angeles, invited to appear on "Disneyland's 35th
Anniversary Celebration," performing a rap version of
"Supercalifragilisticexpialidocious."

At home things weren't good, his finances in ruins, his
musical career not rising to the heights he'd hoped for.
There was no real incentive to hurry back to Philly. He
decided to stay in California for a few days, and while he
was there, attended a taping of "The Arsenio Hall Show"
(as a VIP guest, of course). That particular episode was a
tribute to one of the great arrangers and producers, Quincy
Jones, a man who'd shaped so much great music. Will was
honored to meet him.

But the big moment occured later, out in the parking lot,
when Will asked directions to his next stop—an L.A. Lak-
ers game—from a man named Benny Medina.

Medina was also African-American, still young, and vice
president in charge of Black Music at Warner Bros. Records. Quite naturally he knew who he was talking to; in
fact they'd met once before. With a number of common
interests, they began to chat.

"I met [Benny] and his partner a few years ago and I
saw them again at Arsenio Hall's show," Will recalled in
Jet. "He told me he had this idea he wanted to do." The
idea intrigued Will enough to arrange to meet Medina later,
where they could discuss it in more detail.

Essentially, Medina wanted to put his young life on television. Although he was a powerful executive these days,

he'd started out with any number of disadvantages, the son of a single mother, living in Watts. When his mother died, he spent several years moving in and out of juvenile centers and foster homes, with a very incomplete education. For all intents and purposes, it looked as if Medina was being guided straight towards the underclass.

When he was fifteen, all that changed. It was another foster home, but one that was totally different from anything he'd ever experienced—in Beverly Hills, the house of Jack Elliot and his family. Elliott was a composer whose work appeared in movies and television. His friends were the rich and famous of the time.

"I literally put on a backpack and rode my bike to their home in Beverly Hills," Medina said. "I never left." The black Medina became part of the white Elliot family.

"My deal was that I had to maintain good grades, keep a job, and respect the household. I was kind of an aggressive, smart-ass kid coming into a place where they had such a completely different background. I could never figure out how I was going to exist in that household."

But his experiences there completely altered his life. Now Medina was very much a part of the black middle class, and able to look back. What he saw in his past would make a great sitcom, he thought. And with Will Smith, he believed he'd met exactly the right person to star in it.

Will was certainly open to suggestions.

"He's never been one to stay in one place," was Jeff Townes's assessment. Indeed, going back to their first days together, Will had told Jeff that he "wanted to be in movies."

There were big bills to be paid, Will was needing money from somewhere, anywhere, and the music wasn't much of a challenge any more. So when he and Medina sat down for a more extensive discussion, and he heard the idea in full, Will let it be known that he was very interested indeed.

Now Medina had a name, and that was a start. The next step was a producer, and he had one in mind. He met with

Quincy Jones, who'd gone on become something of a power broker in Hollywood.

Jones liked Medina's idea, and he, too, was familiar with Will from his records and videos. He knew full well that there was a dearth of good black shows on television—"The Cosby Show" had been the only one to give a really positive portrayal to blacks—and that this could be exactly what was needed.

Less than a month after Will and Benny had met in the parking lot, Jones and Medina were pitching the idea of a sitcom to the late Brandon Tartikoff, head of NBC Entertainment, with Will Smith as its star. Jones had sent Tartikoff a copy of the "Parents Just Don't Understand" so he could see for himself the friendly, goofy charisma that Will projected onscreen. From just those few minutes, Warren Littlefield, president of NBC Entertainment, was convinced of Will's talent.

"It was clear to me right away that this guy was a natural. I would go up and down the halls saying we had to do something with him."

Sitting around a table filled with NBC executives in Burbank, Medina explained his idea. Tartikoff's only comment, as he ushered Jones and Medina out, was "Hmm, cute life."

But the next day the phone rang in Jones's office. It was Tartikoff. NBC wanted the show—with Will. It was exactly what they'd been searching for, one which could tap into not only the family audience but also, through the presence of Will Smith, the teens, both black and white, who were getting into hip-hop in droves. The only modification was that instead of Will joining a white family in Beverly Hills, they should be black. Both Jones and Medina could live with that.

There was only thing remaining, and it was really nothing more than a formality. No one had taken the time to see if Will could really act.

"At the time I thought, 'Why not do TV?'" Will said later. "I was sooo cocky."

He was called in for an informal audition at Jones's home (which was in Bel Air), in front of the NBC executives. Although he'd never acted, and was there on two days' notice, "I wasn't scared because I knew this was what I had to do. I had scheduled readings for "Cosby" and "Different World" but I didn't go to them. I was scared. I was making excuses. But when this came up I said to myself: 'This is my shot. I'm taking whatever happens.' This was my thing and I was going to do it."

Will spent a few minutes rehearsing out of sight. Facing everbody, he was decidedly nervous.

But, said Warren Littlefield, "There were no beads of sweat. Will read from a script and nailed it. I sat there thinking, Whoa! Just bottle this guy!"

And as Medina remembered it,

"Will read the script, put some of his personal nuances in it, and right after that everybody was shaking hands, hugging and kissing." And later he would add that "I realized I had just sat through one of those moments that people always talk about having."

The contracts were signed on the spot. Will was going to have his own primetime sitcom. The only thing was, it felt rather like the emperor's new clothes to him. Everybody had wanted him to succeed so much that it would have been virtually impossible to fail. Before he'd walked out in front of them, he'd believed he could act. After doing it, he knew he couldn't. They were going to make him into a star, have him head up a cast of talented actors, and he simply couldn't act.

"I was wondering at the beginning why no one asked if I could act," Will said. "Not Quincy, not NBC. Nobody. They even shot the pilot and never asked me: 'Can you act?' "

The basic reason, of course, was that it didn't matter. NBC could smell a hit show and they wanted it before anyone else had the chance to grab it. Whether he could act or not, it was obvious that Will had star quality. Anything beyond that would have been a bonus, the icing on the cake. As it was, if they surrounded him with real actors, his failings would be less apparent—he could still carry the show on his personality. Will was like the little boy at the parade, thinking that the emperor was naked; for the moment, though, he kept his mouth shut about it. He was new, he was still very green to the ways of the biz, and he didn't want anyone thinking he was getting above himself.

Besides, there was too much work to be done in too little time to think about anything as trivial as acting lessons. Having agreed in January to do a series, the concept still had to be firmed up, a pilot written, cast, and filmed, and then work had to begin without any delay on the first season. NBC wanted it to air in September.

So while work went on behind the scenes, Will had to return to Philadelphia, pack up his worldly goods—although broke, he'd managed to retain quite a few—and move back across the country to Los Angeles.

The blow of being so far from his family was eased by the fact that it put him much closer to his girlfriend, Tanya Moore. They'd met the previous year, when Will and Jeff were performing at San Diego State University. The same age as Will, she'd been a senior then, finishing up a business degree. He'd noticed her in the crowd, and once their set was over, according to Moore, "came up and said I was the girl of his dreams." Even as the money madness continued, then rapidly dried up, they continued to date—she was one reason he'd been glad to come out and tape that Disney special. When he moved to the West Coast, Tanya, now graduated and studying for a real estate license, moved into Will's Burbank apartment. For him she seemed like the perfect companion, definitely female, but with enough of a tomboy side for Will to always feel comfortable around her.

"We just hang out," he explained. "What's good about Tanya is that she thinks like a guy, so I don't miss my buddies. It's like, I can't relate to somebody crying because she broke a fingernail."

One thing Will was quite determined not to do was "go

Hollywood.'' NBC might be making him into a star, but he was still the kid from Philly—and after all, wasn't that the whole idea? Still only twenty-one, he'd learned a lot about life very quickly, and he was going to make sure that this time around his feet stayed firmly on the ground, even if his head was up in the clouds. There'd be no trendy restaurants for him.

"What do you go there for? Avocado pizza?'' he wondered. "No way! You'll never catch the Fresh Prince eating an avocado pizza! I'd rather go to McDonald's. . . . My theory is, just don't try to adjust. When you try to do that, that's when you have problems. Let L.A. adjust to me.''

That more or less echoed the advice that Will had been given just after he arrived. No sooner was he settled in his apartment than the phone rang and, ''. . . Eddie Murphy invited me up to his house. And I'm, *Wow!* I'm going to Eddie Murphy's house.''

Murphy was friendly, funny, and charming, then he turned serious and said to Will:

"There's three things that you're gonna hear, and if you can ignore these three things, you'll be fine. They're gonna say you're gay, you're broke and you're on drugs. Everybody in Hollywood, that's what they write.'' Learn to accept this, Murphy insisted, "and you can deal with everything else you have to deal with in Hollywood.''

Of course, Will *was* broke—it was one of the turns of fortune that had landed him in a television series. But the point was well taken.

Needless to say, the original idea of Medina's underwent more than a few changes once it reached the creative people. NBC had already said they wanted their main character living with a wealthy black family. And to keep it a real family show, it wouldn't be a foster home for the Fresh Prince. Instead he'd be a relative, a streetwise kid from Philadelphia, who'd been having problems at home, and ended up being sent west to live with the rich side of the family.

With the concept nailed down, the network brought in writers Andy and Susan Borowitz who had a proven prime-time record. They'd scripted episodes of "Archie Bunker's Place" and "Family Ties." But the young black experience was a little outside their parameters, to the point where Will had to instruct them in the slang and the music.

Then it was time to create the new family. There was Phil Banks (Uncle Phil), a successful lawyer, his wife Viv, and their children Hilary, Carlton, and Ashley. Hilary would be something of a California valley girl type, Carlton all prim and proper, following in his father's footsteps, and Ashley the precocious kid character that seemed to be crucial to the success of all sitcoms. And, just to emphasize how rich the family was, there'd even be an English butler. Finally, the location was changed. Instead of the Beverly Hills where Medina had lived, this would take place in Bel Air.

As far as the casting process went, it was quick and smooth. James Avery would play Phil. With a strong background in television and films, he was a seasoned professional who knew his way around a set. Janet Hubert-Whitten, selected for Viv, had also put in plenty of time on television and movies, as well as appearances on Broadway. Alfonso Ribiero (Carlton) had been in "Silver Spoons" and already been a Broadway star. Karyn Parsons, who became Hilary, had made commercials and had guest appearances in a number of series. Joseph Marcell, cast as Geoffrey the butler, hadn't been seen in America before, but had a long stage resume in England. Even Tatyana M. Ali (Ashley), the youngest member of the cast, had impressive credits; she'd been a professional for six years, working on "Sesame Street," "The Cosby Show," "All My Children," and others, as well as having won "Star Search" twice. The pedigrees everyone brought to the show were long and full.

And then there was Will, with absolutely no acting experience beyond the church plays his grandmother had staged. For him this was the biggest test yet. He'd made it in music, but that was on his own terms. Here was was quite decidedly the amateur in a group of real profession-als—and he was the one who was supposed to carry the show.

That was true in more ways than one. It had already been decided that Will would be playing a character named, inventively enough, Will Smith. Within the context of the show he wouldn't be a famous rapper, although there'd be references to him having being involved with music in the past. And he wouldn't perform on the show (although he did write and record its theme song). He would be the Fresh Prince, not of Philadelphia, but of Bel Air. In other words, in a lot of ways he'd be himself playing himself.

Certainly he prepared hard for the challenge of the pilot episode. If it failed to work, there was every chance that NBC, which had a lot riding on the show, would yank it from the fall line-up.

He learned every line in the episode. Not only his, but those of every other character. He knew the cues, even if he didn't have the training to always hit his mark on the set. He believed he was ready.

And he still thought so, even as the filming began. He knew all the lines, he wasn't going to blow it.

"I remember when they did the pilot," Karyn Parsons said in *TV Guide*. "I was a nervous wreck as I entered my scene, not breathing, scared to death. I turned to Will and started to say my lines and he mouthed them back as I said them."

Will readily admitted his mistake.

"I was trying so hard. I would memorize the entire script, then I'd be lipping everybody's lines while they were talking."

It was an amateur's mistake, but then Will was still very much an amateur. He knew he was bad; he said, "I sucked badly." But when talking to friends after he saw the fin-ished pilot, he played down just how bad, saying, "There were things I could have done better. I missed the rhythm, I didn't quite hit the laughs."

If he was appalling, then the executives at NBC didn't notice. Nor did the selected audience for whom it was previewed. It became NBC's highest-testing comedy ever in its preview, leading Brandon Tartikoff to offer Will the kind of billing he really didn't need at this stage, as the "next Eddie Murphy." Tartikoff gave the green light for an entire season of shows, which meant weeks of frantic, rushed work for cast and crew.

The buzz was out about Will Smith, that he was going to be a star. 20th Century Fox hurriedly signed him to a film deal for two movies. Life was going his way again.

"There is nothing bad about my life," he admitted. "I'm 21 years old. I have a strong, positive attitude, I've got a record career, I've got a TV career, I'm in love, I'm healthy, my family is healthy. . . ."

After the brief, major detour, Will Smith was quite firmly back on track. And he wasn't just going to be star, he would also have the satisfaction of being involved in a show that was doing something good for the black population of America.

"There is a full, wide spectrum of black people," Will said. "There are different types of black people. And everyone is represented on the show. We're showing something that's never been shown on television. We're showing black on black prejudice. It's more of a class thing. My aunt represents the middle. Her husband is snooty and a black Republican."

The idea of black on black prejudice might have been a little extreme, but its comedy began with the juxtaposition of the street and the mansion. And Will would certainly be the first b-boy on primetime, with his clothes, baseball hat, and boom box.

"There was kind of a concern about the unknown," he admitted. "I was one of the first of the hip-hop generation on television, so there was a sense of wonder if it was going to translate, about how America would accept this hip-hoppin', be-boppin', fast-talking kind of black guy."

What it all came down to was would it work? *Could* it work? Will believed so.

"I have a pretty good eye and ear for what Americans will think is funny," he said confidently, but added, "Nobody knows what a runaway hit is until the fans say it's a runaway hit."

As filming for the season began, it became apparent just how unschooled Will was as an actor. He couldn't find his marks; he continued to mouth all the lines, (to the consternation of everyone playing opposite him) and his comic timing needed a lot of work. Still, he was the star, and this was his series, so the others did all they could to work around him and alongside him.

"When I watch those [first] episodes, it's disgusting," Will would say later. "My performances were horrible."

Just how horrible was confirmed by Tatyana Ali, several years Will's junior but a much more seasoned actress.

"I couldn't believe what a bad actor he was. I'd do a scene with him and he would mouth my words while I was doing my lines. . . . If you look at the old shows, you can see it."

"This is really new for me," Will said in his own defense. "I had to learn not to look at the camera. In videos, that's what you do."

Unskilled as his work was, something still managed to shine through. It was quite apparent that Will had charisma, that special quality that money can't buy and can't be taught. It was a true star quality. Certainly Quincy Jones noticed it.

"He is a monster talent," was Jones's judgment. "I know real stars. I've worked with Streisand, Sinatra, Michael Jackson."

Whether it was true or not, at this point Will was struggling; he didn't need that kind of pressure, or the comparisons with Eddie Murphy. He knew that he still had a long way to go. He had a habit of delivering his lines flatly, forcing director Debbie Allen to work with him in order to animate everything. He had to learn to let his voice carry, so the studio audience could hear him. If he'd been a real actor, he'd have been out of a job. Instead, said writer/producer Andy Borowitz, "We are seeing an improvement every day. He has a natural ability [but] it's not like we pulled some schmo off the street."

Will also learned quickly that being the star of a series gave him a certain power. He might not have a title like producer or director, but his name offered clout. He was bringing Jeff Townes out to Los Angeles, so the two of them could work on another album. When he suggested adding him to the cast, first in a guest spot as Jazz, an oafish con artist, which was expanded into a recurring character, the deal was immediately done.

"I'm doing the show from nine to five," Will told *Jet*. "And from six until midnight I'm in the studio working on the album. As long as I get my eight hours of sleep, I'm fine. I don't need a social life. You see, I've got to work now and I'll have a social life when I'm thirty."

The club scene and the parties that were a constant feature of life in the Los Angeles entertainment business held absolutely no attraction for him. And, of course, he had Tanya waiting at home for him in Burbank.

Will had always been focused in his work, and he had a very clear sense of his goals. He wanted the show to succeed, and he wanted the new record (which would be called *Homebase*) to put him back on top. But there were underlying motivations in all his effort. Not only did he have a massive debt to the IRS that needed to be paid off before he could really get on with his life again, but he had something to prove—that having gone from the heights to the depths, he could climb all the way back, to the summit. His competitive streak wouldn't allow for anything less. He needed, quite desperately, to be successful in anything and everything he undertook, to show he was the best and wouldn't be defeated. It was, in other words, the perfect attitude for Hollywood.

* * *

The first show of "The Fresh Prince of Bel Air" arrived on television screens across America on Monday, September 10, 1990. Titled "The Fresh Prince Project" it detailed how and why Will was coming from Philadelphia to this foreign environment, and served to introduce the cast, playing off the distinctly different worldviews of Will and his relatives.

In *Time*, Richard Zoglin wasn't enthusiastic. He pointed out the similarities between "Fresh Prince" and "The Beverly Hillbillies" (which cast and crew openly admitted; in fact, Will's rap, which was the show's theme song, even made reference to it), and while he conceded that "Rapper Will Smith is an appealing star," he found the "rich-folks-get-their-comeuppance plot" cliched and boring.

The New York Times also had reservations about the show, but admitted that, "One inital doubt about the program has already been resolved, however: Mr. Smith not only can sing, write, and dance, he can clearly act, too." And *TV Guide* was also quick to sing his praises, noting "Will Smith's enjoyment of his role is infectious." *Variety* singled him out as "a remarkably proficient actor, mugging mischeviously for the camera with almost palpable charm but also mastering his more serious moments in the script . . . Smith's unusual appeal alone makes [the show] worth watching. The fact that the writing is generally good and the acting even more so is just icing on the cake." Among the pundits, the biggest dissent came from Andy Edelstein in *New York Newsday*. He made a musical analogy: "It's as if, in 1958, NBC wanted to show America that rock-and-roll was safe, and cast a show with Pat Boone instead of performers with more of an edge."

He was entitled to his opinion, even if his analogy wasn't strictly accurate. Boone, who was white, had watered down black music for white consumption, and been very successful at it. Will had been involved in hip-hop for several years, and the music he and Jeff made might have been commercial, but it had never been deliberately diluted for the masses.

However, the critics were one thing; the viewing audience was quite another. Reviewers could utter praise until they ran out of words, but if televisions weren't tuned to a show and ratings were low, then its future would be very limited.

NBC had staked a lot on "The Fresh Prince of Bel Air," and there was plenty of tension around the offices until the ratings appeared. At that point there was jubilation. The show had won its time slot, up against ABC's "Mac-Gyver" and a CBS comedy, "Uncle Buck."

Surprisingly, it was "Uncle Buck" that gave more competition as the season began to unfold. The second week it won the time slot, and victory see-sawed between the two shows. But Will was determined that in the long run he wasn't going to be defeated.

"Aw man," he said, "I'm goin' to fight back. I'm goin' to make sure he never wins again, never!" He wasn't content with things as they were; it was important to him. "When the ball is in the fourth quarter, always take the shot," he said firmly. "I always take the shot."

And while ultimate victory was out of his control—it rested with an audience sitting in their own homes—he did everything he could to make it a reality. There were interviews, photo shoots, personal appearances. During the show's first season he was on 'The Tonight Show" four times promoting it. He was willing to become a machine to make "The Fresh Prince of Bel Air" number one in the ratings; it mattered that much to him.

In the end, he did it. "Uncle Buck" just couldn't keep up its early success. As Will improved, his show got better, and no one else stood a chance. By the end of the season "Uncle Buck" was a cancelled also-ran, and "MacGyver" had never stood a chance from the word go. "The Fresh Prince of Bel Air" was the undisputed champion of eight P.M. Monday.

Will felt justified. He'd done exactly what he set out to do. But no success would be complete without a backlash. And, just as it had when he'd enjoyed runaway chart success with his music, the criticism came from members of the hip-hop community.

On "Yo! MTV Raps," Will was taken to task for the show's "soft, 'Cosby'-like approach to black youth culture." If that meant kids weren't running around with guns, then it was perfectly true. The series had never been intended to show that side of life. It was, just like Will's music, entertainment, aimed at a mass audience. If they started depicting the harsher side of the black experience, no one—and most certainly not the mostly white primetime audience—would watch.

At the same time, Will felt compelled to defend the show.

"I have a lot of opinions," he said. "I agree with things that Chuck D and Public Enemy say, but I have a different way of expressing myself. I like blending a message with comedy so it's subtle. I want people to enjoy themselves, then be left with something subliminally."

In other words, his approach to television was exactly the same as his approach to hip-hop. And it wasn't true at all that "The Fresh Prince of Bel Air" didn't confront issues. By only the sixth episode, in October 1990, the question of prejudice was raising its head. Entitled "Mistaken Identity," it showed what happened when Will and Carlton drove neighbor Henry Furth's expensive car to meet up with the families in Palm Springs. They were stopped by the police, who found it unlikely that two black kids could be legally driving the vehicle, and they were jailed until everything could be resolved.

It was taken from real life—Will himself had been stopped for the same reason more times than he wanted to remember, and it was true for almost every black male who'd ever driven a nice car. It certainly resonated among all the successful rappers, with their BMWs and Jeeps, but few of them bothered to offer praise.

By late October, when the show took an unprecedented step in airing two shows back to back—"Someday Your Prince Will Be in Effect, Parts One and Two,"—it had caught its stride. It was showing just how good it could be, and that the opposition really stood no chance.

The word continued to circulate that the show was a smash, and its performance in the ratings seemed to confirm that. And Will was being hailed as a star.

That was fine, but after his experience of having it all and losing it, this time he was going to approach everything cautiously, taking all the words with a large pinch of salt, and never letting his feet leave the ground.

"Money means too much out here," he observed. "People are *real* on the East Coast."

Some were, some weren't. But he'd taken Eddie Murphy's advice about Hollywood very firmly to heart. While everyone else was raving about his acting, he knew that he still had a long way to go—in fact, that he'd barely begun. But he wanted to show them all he could really do it.

"My motivation is that I hate not being on top. I get mad by being creative."

Being the best, being the first—Will was a little older than the rapper who'd hit so big with "Parents Just Don't Understand," but his motivations continued to be the same. He'd expressed a desire to make the first hip-hop movie, but Kid 'N Play, another duo, had managed to get there before him, making *House Party,* mining a similar territory in the raps and humor to DJ Jazzy Jeff and the Fresh Prince. That he couldn't be the first rankled with Will.

"No matter how good a movie I do, it will always be second."

Of course, at that point he still assumed he'd be making a hip-hop movie when be began his film career at the end of the "Fresh Prince" season.

But there was a long way to go before any of that could happen. The first season of the show did remarkably well in the ratings, but that didn't mean there weren't problems. Will's acting still left a great deal to be desired, although it was true that he was learning and improving every day.

"The only thing that saved me on the show that first

year was the fact that everyone *else* in the cast was funny,'' he admitted.

And inevitably there was some resentment and a few personality clashes. A bunch of seasoned professionals had found themselves playing second bananas onscreen to someone with absolutely no experience in acting or comedy, largely carrying him through several months of work. There were bound to be a few conflicts and some grumbling.

It showed most obviously in the friction between Tatyana M. Ali, the cast's youngest member, and Will; not professional resentment, but simply two people who didn't see eye to eye on a personal level.

''I liked his rap music,'' Tatyana admitted, ''because he was the only rapper my mother let me listen to, but at first we weren't pals.'' Will admitted as much, but thought he understood the real reason.

''That first year Tatyana and I clashed because I felt like her older brother and she wasn't having any of it.''

At least in some ways, everyone really was coming together like a family, with all its ups and downs. Some of it came out as the first season was being wrapped up. It had already been confirmed that they'd all be back for another year—a foregone conclusion, given the ratings—and Will gathered the other actors together.

''Will said to us, 'I'm really mad at you people,' '' James Avery recalled. '' 'You let me get out there on stage and make a fool of myself.' ''

It was the kind of thing he could only say to people he trusted, who were, at least in some fashion, like family. He knew his work hadn't been good enough (later he'd look back and call it ''horrible''), nowhere near as good as theirs, but they'd been afraid to say anything because he was the star. But in his reprimand there was also something of a cry for help, to make him better.

It was something of a quandary. Much of the premise of the show was about Will being Will, as natural and unaffected as possible, reacting as a Philly boy might to this very different lifestyle. But at the same time, Will needed to be able to put himself across on the same level as the others, which required a certain amount of acting.

No one at NBC seemed concerned about his lack of ability and craft. The show was top of its time slot—it wasn't broken, so there was no need to fix it. The person who seemed most upset, but who was really caught in the middle, was Will himself.

During the year, as the awareness had grown on him, he'd given it a great deal of thought. If he was going to do anything, he understood he'd have to do it on his own, and he thought he saw a solution.

He'd signed to do two movies, and in them perhaps, he could acquire the first real glimmers of professionalism. While the studio was probably looking at him as a leading man, he knew that was out of the question for now—if he couldn't carry a television sitcom to his own satisfaction, what chance did he have with a film? But, in small parts he could learn a great deal.

And that was why, during his break from "The Fresh Prince of Bel Air," he ended up with a very minor role in *Where The Day Takes You*.

This was far from comedy, a very real look at homeless kids on the streets of Los Angeles who come together under the leadership of King (Dermot Mulroney). It was about the day-to-day living, the panhandling, sleeping rough on a freeway underpass known as the Hole—the closest most of the kids had to a home.

It was strongly cast, with Lara Flynn Boyle, Kyle Maclachlan (as a slimy drug dealer), Ricki Lake, and Balthazar Getty among the actors. With his rapidly growing fame, Will could probably have had a large part, but instead he took the role of Manny, disabled and confined to a wheelchair.

He couldn't have gone further from the Fresh Prince, both the character and the rapper. But that was precisely the point. He was on the set both to learn and to prove himself, to show the world and himself that he really did have acting ability. More than that, he understood that in its small way, this was an important film.

"Just seeing how people ignore the homeless was an amazing lesson. I was in full makeup on Hollywood Boulevard, and people didn't know me. It was a revelation seeing how cold people could be."

Will's minor part didn't take long to film, but it was long enough for him to absorb a number of lessons, both about movies and acting. It was more than enough to justify what had seemed like an odd, unlikely choice for a movie debut. The only shame was that his performance—or the performances of anyone else in the film—wasn't widely seen.

The movie, with its ultimately depressing subject matter, received very little distribution on its release in 1992, which was a pity. While it wasn't *Streetwise,* the landmark 1984 documentary about homeless teens, it offered a very realistic, unflinching look at the way some kids are forced to live. Indeed, its very realism might well have been the reason it wasn't pushed, since America's conscience wasn't quite ready to be pricked yet. *People* could find no sympathy for the characters, calling them "irresponsibe brats who find the street life romantic and basically prefer having chips on their shoulders to working."

Will had gone into it all with a lot to prove, and he'd come out with full credit. Much of the business of making movies, unlike a television show, was in the set-up, forcing the actors into a hurry up and wait situation. But Will had used his time well, to listen and learn, both from watching and from conversation with his co-workers.

But filling his vacation with the movie served another purpose, too: it kept his mind from dwelling on what had been going on in his personal life. At the beginning of the year he and Tanya had split up. They'd gone from being so perfect together, such an ideal match, to no longer communicating.

Will's reaction was to throw himself even more heavily into his work. With Jeff he was finishing up the new album, there was the first season of "The Fresh Prince of Bel Air" to be wrapped up, followed by shooting on *Where The Day Takes You*. Already something of a workaholic, he plunged in as deep as he could, pushing himself hard to keep the pain of separation at bay.

But what had gone wrong? With remarkable restraint, neither Will nor Tanya ever gave details to the press, but rumors naturally circulated. She'd got tired of just sitting at home while Will was busy working all the time and wanted a real life of her own—which meant away from him. More gossip let it be known that she'd begun to date singing star Johnny Gill, of New Edition.

The closest Will ever came to revealing all was when he said, "When I got famous, women started looking at me differently. The girl I was with, no matter how much we were in love, just couldn't accept the fact that other women were looking at me and screaming at me onstage. And love just couldn't beat life, not in my situation."

Whatever the reason, it was over, and Will was emotionally devestated by it. Tanya had been his first adult girlfiend, the first person he'd lived with, really shared his life with, and it wasn't a step he'd taken lightly. For all his playful attitude, he was quite serious about romance and matters of the heart. He'd had high hopes of things continuing and growing with Tanya. He was still young, his popularity was increasing every week, but he was, as he'd always been, not the kind of person who ever wanted to play around and sample the female goods that were very definitely on offer to him.

"There's probably only four women in Los Angeles that have intimate knowledge of Will Smith," he'd say several years later. "You know, I had my brief period, a short time in my life, but that got old real quick. I want to love somebody. I just always prefer one woman. The intimacy is so much more enjoyable when it's with someone you love. Because I know I can pretty much have sex with anyone I choose, it becomes less appealing. It's no challenge. A successful relationship is much harder than sleeping with as many woman as you can.''

Seeking love and an ongoing relationship would soon lead him to someone else. But at the same time, he wasn't going to let his heart and its loneliness get in the way of his professional life. He was already quite adept at separating the two, and he knew that he had to concentrate on his career. Or careers, since the new album was finished and ready for release.

CHAPTER FOUR

I am a rapper. I will *always* be a rapper.''

In the light of the success of ''The Fresh Prince of Bel Air'' it was perhaps necessary for Will Smith to say that. He might have initially come to fame for his music, but one season on television had changed that. Now most of America knew him for his comedy. But he hadn't deserted hip-hop, and he hoped it wouldn't desert him.

Homebase was the record Will and Jeff Townes had spent their nights working on while their days (particularly Will's) were occupied on the set in Burbank. It was a relief, an escape from the pressure of making a TV series—the perfect way to still be creative and let off steam.

DJ Jazzy Jeff and the Fresh Prince picked up exactly where they'd left off two years before with *And in This Corner*. Hip-hop had become much darker, with West Coast gangsta rap either reflecting life on the street or glorifying guns and violence, East Coast rap becoming more and more political. The duo were a breath of fresh air, some light relief among all the seriousness.

They hadn't lost their touch in moving to Hollywood. The rhymes were as sharp as ever, and, if anything, Jeff had increased his skill on the decks. And certainly sales wouldn't be hurt by the fact that Will—or at least the Fresh Prince—was, quite literally, well on his way to being a household name. The fact that the music didn't disappoint was the icing on the cake.

If the album contained one standout track, it had to be ''Summertime.'' Not a remake of the old jazz standard, it was about the joys of just hanging out on a hot summer's day, going to the park, watching the girls. Released as a single, and pushed by a video that jumped into immediate heavy rotation on MTV, it rocketed up the charts, carrying the album in its wake. Now Will was very definitely a double threat.

The success reaffirmed him. Will's need to be the best at everything he undertook had only increased after his first season on television. He knew that he could become the equal of anyone else there, but it would take time and patience. In music, though, he'd done it before, and the comeback gave him exactly the confidence he needed to begin the second season.

According to Will, the acting advice he was still receiving from Quincy Jones was to "just do what I'm doing. He told me that if a blind man is walking in the right direction, you don't stop him."

And Will was moving in the right direction. But, like the blind man, he was feeling his way along and moving very slowly—too slowly for his own tastes. However, there was very little he could do about it yet. As the star he had some power and clout, but not that much. The formula and chemistry in the show seemed to be working fine; since nothing appeared to be broken, no one wanted to fix it.

He was still being touted as the next Eddie Murphy, a title he didn't want and knew he didn't deserve—yet. Eddie had become a friend, and he knew that it wasn't Will himself making the comparisons, but Will still felt obliged to publicly apologize for them. He had the potential, but he knew it was still "four or five years" away.

In spite of the shortcomings Will acknowledged, "The Fresh Prince of Bel Air" performed even better than it had in the first season. It had become the successor to the family mantle worn by "The Cosby Show," but with a slightly different emphasis. It could range from the fairly serious—interracial marriage or PSAT scores—to the ridiculous—Will's nightmares about doctors on the eve of having his tonsils removed. That particular show brought in as guest stars both Bernie Kopell, who'd played the doctor on "The Love Boat," and another doctor, rapper Dr. Dre (an interesting inclusion, since on the surface he seemed allied with the hardcore hip-hop community that had always been so critical of Will).

And there were also the heartwarming family stories, such as the Christmas episode. The whole Banks clan went on a Christmas vacation to a Utah ski resort, only to be robbed of all their presents, every single bit of season cheer, at gunpoint.

"What I really like about this particular episode is having the family together," Will explained. "We have a great cast. I like what the audience receives from seeing the family together. The point of this episode is that there aren't any monetary gifts. They've all been stolen. The gifts have been removed but the heart and the thought that originally went into the gifts is still there."

The show was definitely gathering speed. During the first half of its second season, it was finishing fourteenth out of eighty primetime shows. But that wasn't good enough for Will.

"I'm happy about that, but my goal is number one," he announced. "Last year I didn't know anything about television, the audience, etc. . . . We have a new executive producer, Winifred Hervey-Stallworth and she has taken the show into a lot more family-oriented directions, a more socially oriented show. There's nothing, I think, that can keep us from getting to number one."

Those were high aims, but quite typical of Will's need to constantly prove himself, to come out on top. He remained as driven as ever, not only in his desire for the show to be the best, but also for it to have worthwhile content. During the first season the producers had steered away from anything even vaguely controversial, including a proposed show dealing with teen pregnancy. Will was hoping that the second season would see these issues addressed, under the leadership of the new executive producer.

Unfortunately, that wasn't quite going to be the case. In

aiming for a family audience, Hervey-Stallworth kept controversy in the storylines at bay, trying to make ''The Fresh Prince of Bel Air'' a ''classic'' comedy, despite the fact that it had the capacity to cover both bases, largely by virtue of Will himself.

Nor did it finish number one in the ratings. Will might have aspired to that, but the likelihood of it ever happening was slim. It was hugely popular, enough to thrill NBC and make it the anchor of the network's night, but it never stood much of a chance of toppling the real heavyweights.

And, to be fair, Will did have a little more on his mind than just the show. In the wake of Tanya Moore, he'd met someone new.

Her name was Sheree Zampano, she worked as a designer, and they'd met through a mutual—but never named—friend who was in the cast of ''A Different World.'' The pair of them had individually been in the audience for a taping of the sitcom early in 1991—Sheree was actually seated next to Tanya—then had gone backstage afterwards, where they were introduced.

It was Will who was initially smitten, in part because of Sheree herself, and in part, perhaps, because he was on the rebound from Tanya. He'd later say that, for him, it was love at first sight. The feeling was definitely not mutual.

The furthest Sheree would go was giving Will her phone number, and he used it often, calling, talking, asking her out. Still, it would be six months before they finally began dating.

''But I knew,'' Will said. ''You know how you can feel it? When your charm is, like, overpowering someone and they can't defend themselves? And every attempt that they make to keep themselves from falling just makes them fall farther?''

Once they did begin dating, Sheree's resistance crumbled completely, and she found herself won over by Will's easy charm and humor. The relationship quickly moved from friendship to romance. And Will hoped that marriage would soon be on the cards. In fact, as the holidays came, he was staking a lot on it.

"It was Christmas Eve," he recalled. "She was in Los Angeles and she thought I was flying to Philadelphia to spend Christmas with my family. What I actually did was go to the airport to meet my brother. He had flown in specially just to bring me a diamond ring I'd bought from a friend back East. I got the ring and went home. Then I called Sheree, pretending I was still at the airport. I told her I'd forgotten some really important papers. Could she go to my L.A. home, grab them, and bring them to me at the airport? She agreed, but of course, when she got to my house, there I was with the ring. I got down on one knee and proposed."

She said yes, and the couple set a date for May, when "The Fresh Prince of Bel Air" would have finished taping for the season.

But that was still five months away, and Will had plenty to do in between. It would all begin in February, when he and Jeff Townes would receive their second Grammy for the Best Rap Performance by a duo or group during 1991, for "Summertime." That kept them very much at the head of the hip-hop pack, at least in the very conservative view of the Grammy committee.

That award, however, did lead to some tension on the set of the TV show. Foolishly—maybe he didn't really expect to win—Will had promised the cast that if he got a second Grammy, he'd take them all to Hawaii. He won, returned to work, and nothing was mentioned. People waited for tickets, for him to make some mention of it, but there was nothing. And nothing, and nothing.

Eventually they found themselves reminding Will that he'd given his word, and he realized they weren't going to let it drop. So two years later, after the season wrap, he paid for them all to go to Maui. Late, yes, but better late than never.

But a Grammy was only one of the trophies he'd walk away with during 1992. At the NAACP Image Awards, he and Jeff were again honored as Outstanding Rap Artists, and "The Fresh Prince of Bel Air" won for Best Comedy Series. And Will himself was nominated for a Golden Globe in the Best Performance by an Actor in a Television Series category, although he failed to win.

Between all that and his impending marriage, it seemed like Will had a charmed life, that he simply couldn't do any wrong. But he wasn't just letting it happen to him; he was planning ahead.

After *Where The Day Takes You* he knew he was ready to do more on the big screen, to increase the size and scope of his roles. His television work had improved during the second season. Partly it was experience, but he'd also learned a great deal on the movie set.

In fact, he'd been doing a lot of thinking about his career. Even before he walked up to the podium to receive his Grammy he'd been wondering how much longer he'd be involved with music, given the committments in his life.

"I don't want to feel I'm neglecting it," he said. "If I can't do it right, I'd rather not do it."

The future, he realized, lay in television, and even more in movies, although he intended to lay the groundwork properly for that. And there was marriage rapidly looming on the horizon. Workaholic though he was, there was a limit as to how thinly Will could spread himself and still create good work.

And music seemed to be the thing that could go most easily. *Homebase* had done exceptionally well, but the truth was that hip-hop was moving out of his orbit. It was growing and evolving as a form, and he and Jazzy Jeff were no longer on the cutting edge the way they'd been in 1988. It was still enjoyable to go into a studio, to write and make a record, but the satisfaction wasn't what it had once been. Their contract called for one more album, but beyond that he had his doubts—at least in the short-term.

There was one more reason for wanting to cut back— albeit only a little bit—on his activities in the future: Sheree was pregnant. The news wouldn't be released publicly until after the wedding, but she was expecting a baby in the fall. For Will, who was very traditional in his idea of family and parental responsibility, that meant being around to spend time with his son or daughter.

It also meant doing as much work as he could before the birth. Wanting to expand on his film work, he'd put himself up for a role in a comedy, *Made in America*. It was set to star Whoopi Goldberg and Ted Danson, then America's highest-profile interracial couple off-screen.

It wasn't his first choice, however. He'd already talked about roles in *Biofeed*, a science-fiction film, and *Scout*, a baseball movie. But both those projects had been cancelled by the studios.

Although he'd played comedy on television, being funny on the big screen was a completely different challenge, as he understood in great detail.

"Watch Jim Carrey, Tom Hanks, Robin Williams or Eddie Murphy, who all come from comedy television where you learn to maximize every one-hundredth of a second. These guys know that when you do a half hour of television, probably nine minutes of it are yours and that's it. From the first season of 'Fresh Prince' on, I got hold of every TV show and every movie those four guys made, and I watched them over and over to see the differences between the two mediums. . . . Everything in movies is just a touch smaller, a touch slower, because the camera does more of the work in a film."

This was someone who was clearly taking things very seriously indeed, and who'd come a long way from the Will Smith who'd lucked his way through the first episodes of his series on his goofy charm alone. At work was a penetrating intelligence which was able to analyze what was going on, and how to use it.

The producers of *Made in America* were happy to include him in their cast. As with *Where The Day Takes You,* Will had only sought a small role, in this case playing Tea Cake Walters, the hopeful boyfriend of Nia Long's character.

As taping for the second season of "The Fresh Prince of Bel Air" concluded, ending up nineteenth in the overall prime time ratings, he headed up to San Francisco for the movie's location shooting.

While, in comparison, Whoopi Goldberg and Ted Danson were much bigger stars, and more recognizable names, it was Will who brought the fans out. Between takes and when he had breaks from filming, Will was more than happy to give them his attention, signing autographs and posing for photographs. He'd wanted stardom, and now that he had it, he fully accepted the responsibility involved to his audience.

But there was plenty on his mind, most immediately his wedding to Sheree. There'd been a great deal of planning, and no expense was spared—the eventual bill would be in the region of $50,000. Held at the Four Seasons Hotel in Santa Barbara, the reception was for 125 people, including among the glitterati Jeff Townes, Magic Johnson's wife, Cookie, and Denzel Washington—Will was flying with some high company.

No sooner were the nuptials complete than the couple announced Sheree's pregnancy, with Will overjoyed at the impending event.

"Sheree's going to have my baby—and I'm very, very proud of her," he told the *National Enquirer*. "This is the most exciting thing, our baby is going to be a real life fresh prince or princess of Bel Air."

Now he could be gleeful in public, rather than just in private. Everything seemed to be going smoothly. His debt to the IRS had been paid, he was on his way to becoming a rich man for the second time—but definitely not spending it all, and making sure his taxes were taken care of immediately—and now he was going to have a family.

And his career was moving up. "The Fresh Prince of Bel Air" was among the most popular programs in America, which made Will one of the most popular stars in America—an unusual position for someone who was black. On television, possibly only Bill Cosby had previously achieved that. And, like Cosby, Will came across as very non-threatening.

The nature of the medium was that it aimed at a white audience. Rightly or wrongly, that was the networks' target, because, in the eyes of the advertisers, they were the people who had the money to spend. What both Will (indeed, the show itself) and Cosby represented was the black middle class, which was growing rapidly, even as it remained largely unacknowledged. The "buppies" (black urban professionals) were everywhere.

And yet shows that portrayed African-Americans in a positive light (as opposed to the type of black sitcoms on Fox, or those which would appear later on other upstart networks, which seemed designed to play into stereotypes) were still few and far between.

No one, least of all Will, would deny there was still racism in America. At times it was on the surface, at other times it floated just below, but it was never gone completely. When the police stopped him for driving an expensive car, when someone questioned his right to be sitting in first class on an airplane, it was there.

So when Will had an opportunity to be involved in a film that said something about racism—indeed, about prejudice of many kinds—he pursued it.

However, his motives weren't entirely altruistic. In a dramatic role, and as the movie's central character, he'd be stretching himself, taking himself into areas he'd never been before. It was exactly the kind of challenge he needed for himself.

Six Degrees of Separation had been adapted as a screenplay from John Guare's play of the same name. The play was based on factual events that had occured a decade before, when a young black con man had managed to scam white families on two separate occasions. And not just any white families, but people of wealth and social prominence—John Jay Iselin, then president of PBS station WNET, and Osborn Elliott, who was then the dean of Columbia University's Graduate School of Journalism.

He'd appeared at the doors of their Manhattan apartments, with a tale of being a classmate of their sons' at Harvard, and giving his name as Paul Poitier—the son of Sidney Poitier, the famous and highly regarded black actor.

He'd been mugged on the street and had no money, he claimed, and had only come for help because the son had given him the family's address.

Well spoken, dressed in a suit and tie, he seemed perfectly plausible, and in both instances the families invited him in. "Paul Poitier" had done his research very carefully. He knew plenty about the families, the kind of facts their sons' friends might well know.

In both cases he became an overnight guest, accepted and befriended. On one of the nights, once the family was asleep, he slipped out and returned with another man, a male hustler; the two were found in bed together the next morning.

Of course, he wasn't Sidney Poitier's son; Poitier didn't even have a son. And he wasn't a student at Harvard. The con man, whose real name was David Hampton, had constructed an entirely fictional character. In the end he did pay a price for what he'd done, spending 21 months in jail.

But the factual incident raised a number of interesting questions that Guare addressed in his play. There was the implicit racism—"Poitier" was accepted because of his speech and his clothes as "one of them," a member of a privileged elite. And on another level, there was the reaction to homosexuality, when he was discovered in bed with another man.

Guare himself adapted his play for the screen, focusing on just one of the two incidents. Casting for the New York couple went relatively smoothly, with Donald Sutherland and Stockard Channing being chosen, both well-known and respected actors. For the part of Paul Poitier, though, it was altogether a different matter.

Naturally, it appealed to Will, who could see some resonaces of his own situation in the script.

"I meet people every day [to whom] I would just be

another nigger if I didn't have a TV show," he said. "It's like, 'Well, I wouldn't let just any black guy into my house. But Will Smith, he's okay. He's a good black guy.' That's just something you learn to deal with."

But learning to deal with it wasn't the same as being happy about it. And if he could get the part, he felt there was a lot he could bring to it from his own experience, as well as being able to get some of the anger out of his system.

"It's almost like I take off the weight vest of racism when I leave [America]," he told a reporter, "and when I come back through customs I have to put it back on, carry this 150,000 pound weight around every day, just driving around."

What stood in his way was the public perception of Will Smith as a goofy comic actor. He could point to his role in *Where The Day Takes You*, but that was miniscule. Could he carry something like this?

"My drive was the fact that they didn't want me. They didn't think I could do it. They thought I was the *worst* choice you could have for the role."

CHAPTER FiVE

NATURALLY, being the unlikeliest choice gave Will all the ammunition he needed. A few people were in his corner, primarily because he was a "name," but director Fred Schepisi wasn't convinced. He interviewed a large number of actors, none of whom seemed right, before giving in to Will's persistence and agreeing to audition him.

Will had given the situation a great deal of thought. He'd already met Guare, and the writer believed he was perfect for the part, so he had at least one ally. Will knew there was much involved with the role that he couldn't do immediately, so he decided, for the audition, to latch on to those elements that were a part of him and play them to full advantage.

So he arrived in a three-piece suit, convincingly dressed in Brooks Brothers style as a successful Ivy-Leaguer, and then proceeded to turn on the Will Smith charm.

At that point, said Schepisi, "Everybody got excited about Will, but I was a little more cautious. . . . But Will tried to convince me that he'd do whatever it would take, would go through whatever process, was sure he could get himself prepared. That confidence and charm was everything the character should be. [He was] worth taking a chance on."

Another decisive factor might well have been the fact that, according to Will, the film's financial backer (Arnon Milchan, who'd been one of the producers of *Made in America*) was completely taken "with my energy and attitude. He told the company he wouldn't finance *Six De-*

grees of Separation if I didn't have the lead role.''

And so Will was cast. That didn't mean, however, that he was ready to walk into the part. What Schepisi saw was the raw material—plenty of charm and confidence, and some acting ability—but it still needed to be molded. Will needed to learn to use his acting ability—to really learn how to act, in other words—and to be able to speak like a Harvard student. So Schepisi insisted that for three months before filming began, Will work with acting and dialect coaches.

''Will has a reputation and a name, but this was a work of more substance. We weren't expecting to teach him about the whole acting experience,'' Schepisi said, ''but we wanted him to have a healthy respect for what's involved.''

There was never any doubt that Will would agree. This was a role he desired, that he felt could be the making of him, and he wanted to approach it properly.

And working with an acting coach would stand him in good stead when he returned for the new season of ''The Fresh Prince of Bel Air.'' He knew he possessed some innate talent as an actor, but it was still completely unfocused, leaving him to largely coast on his charm. That was fine, but how long could it last? From the very beginning of the show he'd wondered why no one had questioned his acting ability, and although he'd come a long way, he knew he still fell far short of his colleagues on the show. This would give him the chance to acquire some skills, which could only stand him in good stead for the future. He was obviously now quite committed to acting as a career.

If he could pull this off, then he would be accepted as a real actor. As he put it, ''Spike Lee and Spielberg and the big boys will want to work with me,'' showing that, if anything, his ambition was increasing.

But first he had to pull it off, and that was going to be an enormous challenge. As far as the racism went, Schepisi felt that ''. . . Will had a certain amount of identification with the character.'' Playing a gay man would be a different matter altogether.

"Not only is he a homosexual," Will pointed out, "he's a homosexual with jungle fever. He only likes white guys. But that is the aspect of the film that will sell me as an *actor*."

Others had their doubts. Will was woken at four one morning by an old friend calling from Philly. The night before he'd gone to see a stage production of *Six Degrees,* and had been surprised when Poitier and his lover kissed onstage.

"He just wanted to call to make sure I wasn't going to be kissing any men!" Will said.

But, according to the script, that was exactly what he was supposed to do, and be naked and in view while he did it.

That was a hurdle, but it was something Will was confident he could do. First there was the rigor of his preparation. He went to see three different productions of the play around the country, and, as well as his acting and dialect coaches, began spending time with a personal trainer. He buffed up his body to make Paul Poitier more physically attractive, rather than the tall, skinny weed that was Will.

One thing Will had learned to keep under control was his very buoyant personality. Within a television series, he could let it loose, even on the set, but with a film everything had to be absolutely professional—something he'd learned from Whoopi Goldberg while making *Made in America.* Clowning around was fine between takes when you weren't needed, but once the director was ready to get down to business, you had to be serious.

Even so, it didn't stop one small gaffe as the filming of *Six Degrees of Separation* began.

"Will is used to driving the set on 'Fresh Prince' and keeping up enthusiam," Schepisi recalled. "On the first day, just before a take, he let out some wild yells and clapped his hands. He was deafening the sound people and everyone else around him. Finally, Donald [Sutherland] took him aside."

It was a way of psyching himself up, but once told, he never did it again.

"I have this childish energy that manifests itself in noise," Will admitted. "Donald just grabbed my hand and kissed me on the cheek and said, 'Shut up.' That was cool. I'm totally fine with someone who says, 'I think it's time to work now.' "

Often, during breaks, Will and Schepisi would move to a quiet corner. While the assumption was that they were going over lines, or Schepisi was offering direction on upcoming scenes, the truth of the matter was that they had an ongoing chess battle, which, even when filming ended, remained unresolved.

But the question of "the kiss" was still weighing heavily on Will's mind, and he began to wonder if he would actually be able to do it.

"At the beginning of the film, Fred Schepisi and I talked about it," Will told *The Advocate*. "People think it was a last-minute thing. No. From the beginning of the film, the director and I discussed it, and I told him I was a little uncomfortable with that scene, and he said 'Don't worry about it. Let's get started. You've got a lot of other things to worry about, and that's not a huge part of the film. I'll talk you through it when we get there. You're an actor. This doesn't have anything to do with you.' "

And it was true that Will had plenty to think about on the set. Every day was offering new challenges to his ability, and one of the hardest was performing a six-page monologue on-camera, which was "kind of scary...." Memorizing it was difficult enough ("It almost made me not want to take the role"), but executing it was even harder. While Will had been the featured character in a television ensemble, this was the first time he'd been involved in anything which really focused on a character he was playing. The pressure was relentless, with the monologue standing as the single hardest segment. The weeks of coaching helped him through, helped him understand what he was doing, but he still had to draw on resources within himself that he hadn't known existed, let alone understood. And that was especially true when he had to emphasize the gay aspects of his character.

"That was really difficult," he admitted. "I had enough innate charm for the audience to make them buy that this guy could put one over on people. But the gay part—just the concept of looking at a man the way you'd look at a woman and saying to a man what you'd say to a woman— was really hard. I don't have anything against homosexuals—I'm just not one. So there was nothing I'd learned as an actor or done in my life that I could draw on."

Of course, as an actor, Will should have been able to translate the heterosexual experience to the homosexual character, and finally that's what he did. What he thought he'd learned about acting during two seasons on "The Fresh Prince of Bel Air" proved to be nothing but a tiny preamble to the education he was getting in this movie. He'd chosen to plunge into the deep end with very little preparation, and now he was quickly learning the basics. He had no choice; it was either that or drown.

Or perhaps just splash helplessly at times. That was what it came down to with the final shot of the movie, the kiss. Both Will and Schepisi had been putting it off as long as possible, but now there was no delaying it any further. Will, naked except for a "ball pouch" was supposed to kiss Anthony Michael Hall. He'd been wrestling with his demons for the entire length of filming, even going so far as to ask Denzel Washington for advice.

Washington reportedly replied, "Don't be kissing no man," although he would later deny ever having said that.

Even as he prepared for the scene, Will wasn't sure he could actually do it—it just went too much against his nature.

"The director said, 'Don't worry, you're an actor, just get through it.' I said, 'You're going to have to work something else out.' "

In the end it was shot from a different angle, giving the

impression, if no longer the fact, that Will and Hall were kissing.

At the final hurdle Will had failed as a serious actor. At the time his decision made sense to him, but soon he was angry at himself for it.

"It was immature on my part," he admitted. "I was thinking, 'How are my friends in Philly going to think about this?' I wasn't emotionally stable enough to artistically commit to that aspect of the film. In a movie with actors and a director and writer of this caliber, for me to be the one bringing something cheesy to it. . . . This was a valuable lesson for me. Either you do it or you don't."

At twenty-four, and on his way to being a parent, Will still had some growing up to do. That he'd come a long way was obvious, but so was the fact that he still had a ways to go. But it was something he realized himself.

For once, though, he wasn't criticized by others in the hip-hop community for his move. They'd been happy to make negative remarks about his music and his television show, but now that he was playing a gay man, they were all silent.

"Actually it's surprising," Will said. "Everyone applauds me for having the heart to take the role. Rap is about macho, being hard. In a weird kind of way, it turned out that it was a macho and hard thing for me to have the balls to do. I don't know how else to put it. So it's like I couldn't have been more man enough to take this role."

When he finally saw a finished cut of the film, he saw how stupid he'd been, refusing to complete the kiss.

"In the context of the film, it's like it was nothing . . . but at that point it just seemed so huge to me. And I don't know, the frame of mind was wrong."

Will returned from filming a wiser man, and one who had new insight, something to consider and take to heart. Perhaps part of it, in some manner, had been the personal line he'd always toed—never to do anything that would embarrass his mother, and on some level he thought that might have. But, whatever the true reason, it meant that he'd failed himself, and everybody else, at a crucial moment, on a film he saw as very much make or break for the dramatic career he wanted.

At the same time, he felt it had been "the best film experience I could have had. It has encouraged me to make more." And he had plans to do a film a year for as long as his show lasted.

One thing he did need right now was some time with Sheree before he returned to work on "The Fresh Prince of Bel Air." *Where the Day Takes You* had come out, showing him in a slightly different light, and there was also the question of finishing another album with Jeff, the last one left on their contract with Jive Records.

He and Sheree took a trip to Philadelphia. Will needed it to remind him of his roots and to return to the mindset he had to have to play the Fresh Prince again. It was, he understood, getting harder to be that younger character.

"When I started the show, I was pretty much just playing myself, but now my life experience has gone beyond the life experience of the character."

It would take thought and time to readjust. In fact, before he reported back to begin the show's third season, Will watched all the episodes again, trying to recapture the version of himself that was on the small screen. He'd changed in many ways, and with the baby due, he'd be changing in many more. He knew that mere charm wasn't going to cut it anymore. He was going to have to use the skills he'd been acquiring—he was going to have to act.

By his own estimation, it took Will about six weeks back on the "Fresh Prince" set to return to speed. While he was able to focus on his work, there were also a lot of other things on his mind—the baby, the album, and now his film career.

Under the hand of Winifred Hervey-Stallworth the show had definitely changed. As promised, it had become more family-oriented, which was both a good and a bad thing for Will. It didn't try to be the riotous comedy it had been during the first season, but at the same time time it seemed to be avoiding issues Will wanted it to address. Growing older, there was more he'd become aware of in the community—teenage pregnancy, drugs, violence—and by failing to give time to those topics, "The Fresh Prince of Bel Air" was actually insulating itself in an unreal world.

There were some tokens, such as "Momma's Baby, Carlton's Maybe," where Carlton's girlfriend appeared with a baby, insisting Carlton was the father. Of course, he wasn't; he was still a virgin. But Will knew the show could have hit harder.

It wasn't that he wanted to leave the cast; that was the furthest thing from his mind. He simply wanted the show to be truly relevant, and he aired his concerns to the writers, producers, Benny Medina, Quincy Jones, and the people at NBC.

That it could work by taking on real issues was evident by the success of "Roseanne," which hadn't pulled any punches in its portrayal of family life. "The Fresh Prince of Bel Air" could do that, and put its positive messages across with humor, never being didactic.

Naturally, the network was resistant. The show was doing very well as it stood. Why try to make it into something else?

The turning point for Will came when he met Bill Cosby at a party. "The Cosby Show" had been one of the highest-rated shows on television for most of the time it had been shown, and Cosby himself had a reputation as a wise man. Talking to him, Will found himself airing his frustrations about the show.

In many ways they were the thoughts of a young man growing into himself, knowing that he has something to say, but not having an outlet for it. Cosby offered a constructive, creative solution.

"When I complained about the writing on the show, Bill suggested I write a script. 'Just write one and don't go to sleep until it's finished,' he told me." Will followed the advice and found that being critical was easy; actually changing things was a lot more difficult.

"When I met the writers the next day, I had a lot less anger and a lot more understanding of the process," he admitted.

But that didn't mean he was giving up on his quest to make the show better. He still believed that if he was given more control, the show would be able to speak to its prime audience, teens, on their own terms.

In part it was because the show had become familiar ground. He was no longer the rookie he'd been a couple of years before, not knowing anything about how a show was made. And he'd made three movies. He'd genuinely grown as an actor, and as a man. He understood that the show centered around him. That gave him power, and he was finally in a strong enough position to try and exercise it for the good of the show.

Finally he met with Benny Medina and laid out his grievances. It wasn't a power trip or an ego trip. Will's motives were honestly altruistic. He wanted the show to be the best it could be.

Since his name was on the show, figuratively and literally, he was beginning to feel responsibility for the way it developed. But responsibility was on his mind, anyway, with Sheree due to give birth in November. And when the baby was born that would be a responsibility unlike any other he'd had to handle in his life.

Before that, there was a rush for Will and Jeff to complete their album, since there'd be no time afterwards. By the time it was released, two years would have passed since their last record. It was hardly a lifetime, especially considering how busy Will had been, but every day in hip-hop new artists were coming along and displacing those who'd gone before. The built-in advantage of a "name" and the visibility of a television series guaranteed a sales base for the album, to be called *Code Red,* but no one knew how big or small that would be.

In the end, it proved to be smaller than most people had

Jazzy Jeff and the Fresh Prince.
(© Chris V.D. Vooren/Sunshine/Retna Ltd.)

At the Cannes Film Festival.
(© Theodore Wood/Camera Press/Retna Ltd.)

At the premiere of *Set It Off*.
(© Steve Granitz/Retna Ltd.)

With wife Jada Pinkett. (© Steve Granitz/Retna Ltd.)

**On the set of
*Men in Black.***
(© Robert Spencer/
Retna Ltd.)

**With son Trey at
the *Men in Black*
premiere.**
(© Paul Smith/
All Action/Retna Ltd.)

hoped, as *Code Red* only sold some three hundred thousand copies, not even enough to earn a gold record. Set against his other albums, it was a failure. But in many ways, Will's heart hadn't been in the making of it. There was simply too much going on in his life. Not only the show, but movies, a new wife, and impending fatherhood—how could he give that much energy to this project and really focus on it? Will seemed to be happy, indeed to thrive, on doing two things at once (a film and the series, the series and a record), but beyond that his creative energies became a bit diffused.

But *Code Red* saw Will and Jeff fulfill their contract, and while sales hadn't come up to expectations, they'd hardly fallen through the basement, either.

For Will, however, it was a signal that maybe it was time to hang up the microphone. Hip-hop had changed beyond all recognition since he began. By the standards of 1992 he was quite definitely old-school and out of date. And in many ways, that was fine with him. He still loved the music; it was what he listened to in his car and at home. It had been his springboard to everything. But he wasn't the same kid who'd started rapping in his bedroom and at parties. He'd grown. He'd conquered that field a number of years before, and now there were plenty of new challenges, personal and professional. The man who'd announced just a couple of years before that he'd always be a rapper was learning that he didn't need to be, and for now, maybe he didn't even want to be.

And in November, almost everything else went out of the window. Sheree gave birth to a boy, who was duly named Willard C. Smith III, and known to one and all as Trey. As an eager father, Will was in the delivery room when he was born; it was the biggest moment he'd experienced in his life.

"When the doctor handed me my son, it was this Big Explosion. Suddenly I felt this huge yoke of responsibility. Being a dad changes everything."

And it changed it all immediately.

"I suddenly realized things had to be different now,

starting on the car ride home from the hospital. I made a vow to stay healthy, eat right, because it's not just for me anymore.''

Will believed he'd given a great deal of thought to being a father, but now his son was a wriggling, crying reality, he understood that whatever he'd thought before meant nothing. He'd been brought up with a good example from his parents, even after they divorced, and he was bound and determined to do the same for his namesake.

''As Trey grows up I hope he'll be proud of my work ethic and how I treat people. I always try to be nice, try to be positive. Children learn by example and I'm trying to set an example for my son. I want to be the world's greatest dad in the eyes of my son.''

Something that Will really wanted was to be around to see his son grow. And that meant he had to balance the workaholic and the family man within himself. ''The Fresh Prince of Bel Air'' was an ongoing event, and his regular paycheck. As he'd already made noises about wanting to be more involved in all aspects of the show, it was impossible for him to back away from any commitments about that. But he did decide that the next summer he wouldn't work on a movie. For all he'd been saying he wanted to do a film every season, the thing to do was to back off for once, even though scripts were now coming to him on a regular basis.

With two movies due in 1993, he could actually afford the respite. He was going to be visible enough, with *Made in America* appearing during the summer, and the big surprise of *Six Degrees of Separation* arriving just before Christmas.

A rest would not only give him the opportunity to recharge his batteries—he had, after all, being going full-tilt since he was eighteen—but, more importantly, allow him a real family life. It was a chance to play with Trey every day, and to actually enjoy the fruits of his success—and what was the point of having everything if you couldn't enjoy it? He was still young, and the movie projects weren't going to stop coming because he took one year off. He had the luxury of being able to wait until just the right one came along.

In the meantime, Sheree began to bring Trey down to the "Fresh Prince" set, to the point where he became a regular young visitor—the youngest visitor, in fact.

The show continued to do well in the ratings, but changes were definitely in the wind. As Will became more vocal in his criticisms, that seemed almost inevitable.

The biggest upheaval was that Andy and Susan Borowitz became completely disassociated from the show. Initially the writers, they'd moved into the position of executive producers, and remained resistant to change, even after Winifred Hervey-Stallworth joined them as an executive producer.

It was the decision to give Will input into the storylines and scripts that changed everything. It altered the balance of creative control in a way that left them unhappy.

"They decided, if that was the case, that they'd rather not continue as producers—which none of us were upset about," was Benny Medina's comment.

And that meant that Will climbed into the suddenly vacant co-producer's chair. With his ambition it was a natural progression, and he had very definite ideas about where he wanted to take the show.

"We're talking about a seventeen-year-old black man from the inner city and there are certain things he should be concerned with—sex and drugs, for two. He should have more involvement with friends from the inner city. There will be lots of touchy issues on the show, like prejudice. I want everyone to be enlightened when they watch our show. We're going to show Americans themselves!"

The changes were set to go into effect with "The Fresh Prince of Bel Air" 's fourth season. It was obvious that there was going to be a difference in the tone and the scripts. What no one involved had anticipated was that there'd also be a change in the cast.

To everyone who watched, Janet Hubert-Whitten *was* Aunt Viv. She'd created the character and taken her through a number of changes. Not the least of those was her own pregnancy, which had been written into the storyline. Everything seemed to be going smoothly. Then, at the end of the third season, her contract wasn't renewed. She learned that she was going to be replaced as Aunt Viv by Daphne Maxwell Reid, the wife of actor Tim Reid, who had strong credentials of her own.

Unsurprisingly, Hubert-Whitten was incensed. And since it had happened after the reins had been handed to Will, she blamed him for her being fired.

"Anyone who stands up to Mr. Smith on 'Fresh Prince' is gone," she told a reporter. "Yes, I reprimanded him constantly for being rude to people and locking himself in his room, but I did not slander him in any way."

Will had little choice but to reply to the charges. In the *Atlanta Journal* he said that she'd been bringing her personal problems onto the set. And in a radio interview he addressed the issue directly:

"I can say straight up that Janet Hubert wanted the show to be "The Aunt Viv of Bel Air Show" because I know she is going to dog me in the press. . . . She has basically gone from a quarter of a million dollars a year to nothing. She's mad now, and she's been mad all along. She said once, 'I've been in the business for ten years and this snotty-nosed punk comes along and gets a show.' No matter what, to her I'm just the Antichrist."

And that, in turn, brought more comments from Hubert-Whitten. In *Jet* she denied ever having made that comment to Will, and asserted, "He probably is responsible for my firing. He has a lot of clout."

Will denied it then, and he was still denying it three years later in *Ebony*.

"That's wasn't me. Janet Hubert-Whitten was an incredible actress. . . . Of course, there was pain in her not returning to the show and all that, but then there was the thing that she thought it was me. That kind of irritated me a little bit, but people will make their own beds, and they are going to have to sleep in them. I didn't have anything to do with it. She just never believed that. I think the show suffered for the loss of Janet Hubert-Whitten.''

By the beginning of 1994 the problem had deteriorated to the point where she filed a lawsuit against both NBC and Will, alleging that she'd been forced off the show after becoming pregnant. The once-happy family would end up in court.

But Will couldn't let that distract him from the show's fourth season. Now he was in a position to influence both the scripts and the set. It was what he'd lobbied for, and he was taking it very seriously indeed.

Most definitely the storylines took a slight turn—not as extreme as he'd wanted. But there was still ''Better to Have Love and Lost It . . .'' where Carlton lost his virginity to an older woman; and ''Home Is Where the Heart Attack Is,'' with Uncle Phil suffering a heart attack and its effect on the family. ''Mother's Day'' had artificial insemination as its topic, and ''Papa's Got a Brand New Excuse'' reunited Will with the father he hadn't seen for fourteen years (played by Ben Vereen).

None of it would really change the way America looked at itself. Will and Carlton had grown, and rather than the problems of adolescence, they were now college students, and facing the world as young men.

Daphne Maxwell Reid managed to slot in as Janet Hubert-Whitten's replacement, and she was full of praise about her treatment.

''These people opened their arms and their hearts. It was like they wanted me there and treated me so well. I came in fresh and uninformed. Now, it feels like I've been part of that family all along. We just have a ball.''

Although it seemed far in the past now, Will's previous summer was just beginning to catch up with him. *Made in America* appeared in theaters, and a number of critics felt that he even stole scenes from Goldberg and Danson, two veterans of comedy. Tea Cake Walters had been a small role, but it had proved that he was more than capable on-screen, a real presence with charisma. And acting ability.

But it was the release of *Six Degrees of Separation* that really put him on the line. Making a serious film that judged peoples' notions about prejudice was a bold move. Since its star was known for television comedy and rapping, it could have been a recipe for disaster.

In the end, reviews were generally favorable. The focus, quite understandably, was on Will. While *The New York Times* felt he lacked "the hints of mockery or desperation that should accompany his deception," most other reviewers were very pleasantly surprised by his performance. Writing in *Variety*, Leonard Klady found him "an extremely charismatic presence, convincing in his sincerity and cunning in conveying his character's talents as a human sponge." *Newsweek*'s assessment was that "Smith, the rapper and star of TV's 'Fresh Prince of Bel Air,' is an eye-opener in a complex, tricky part. Will Smith is going to be big." *Time*, too, offered praise, saying that "As Paul, Will Smith is needy, daring, insinuating," a view echoed by *Entertainment Weekly*, with the opinion that "Will Smith, in an impressive performance, makes [Paul] easy to watch—as smooth and transparent as glass."

He'd taken the risk, and come through with flying colors. Now people had no choice but to see him in an entirely new light. He really could act, given the opportunity, and the reviews made it likely that there'd be more opportunities in the future, whenever he wanted them. But for now there was a show to film, and Will had the executive producer's chair to fill.

CHAPTER SIX

WHY hadn't the show changed more radically? After all, it had seemed like Will's intention was to give it a drastic overhaul and have it be more of a mirror of real life.

One fact he'd learned very quickly in his new position of power was that you didn't make an alteration like that overnight—at least, not when the show was a ratings winner. But since the show was likely to be around as long as Will wanted to be a part of it, things could afford to move more slowly, allowing the American viewing public time to adjust.

Will seemed perfectly content in his new position. And why not? Everything was going his way. He was the star and co-producer of a hit show, and he had a lovely wife and baby. When the season was over he could look forward to a real vacation.

Or perhaps he couldn't. A script came his way that he really wanted to be involved in. *Batman Forever* would introduce the character of Robin. Val Kilmer had already signed on to play the Caped Crusader, replacing Michael Keaton, but his sidekick had still to be cast. If Will could get that part it would be a massive step forward, not only for his career, but for blacks in America.

A publicity campaign wouldn't hurt his chances; after all, he had a higher profile than most of the actors who'd be auditioned, and his name alone would help bring audiences into the theaters. (Not that the movie would necessarily need them—*Batman Returns* had taken in $53 million in its opening weekend, breaking the record set by *Jurassic Park*.) Will told his agent, and even told reporters, that he was actively pursuing the role.

It left those casting the film in a dilemma. Will could probably have handled the role. But would people raised on the comic books accept an African-American Robin? A lot of actors wanted the part. It was tremendous exposure—especially for someone young and unestablished—good money, and there'd almost certainly be sequels.

In the end, they went with Chris O'Donnell, who'd been acting in movies since 1989. He'd really only begun to make a name for himself in 1992, when he was Al Pacino's co-star in *Scent of a Woman*.

It was a blow, to Will as an actor, a star, and a black man. But in the end, perhaps it was only to be expected. Will had proved he had the ability to undertake a dramatic role, but maybe he was too well-known. Certainly he was more of a household name than Val Kilmer, the star, and while big names were brought in to play the villains, for Robin it just wouldn't have worked.

And a black Robin? The idea raised interesting questions. The producers had definitely already altered the DC Comics hero somewhat, making him darker in mood, and giving Gotham City a very noir-ish ambience. But making his assistant African-American would have been an extreme step. Would fans have accepted it? Obviously, that became an academic question, never to be resolved.

To be passed over stung, but at the same time, it was hardly the end of the world. Before this had all happened he'd planned time off, and now he had no excuses. Sheree and Trey were frequent visitors to the television studio in Burbank, but seeing his son in odd moments when he wasn't involved in one thing or another was hardly satisfying. And by the time he made it home in the evening, he was exhausted. Being in a series might have seemed like a nine-to-five job when he'd begun in 1990, but now he was far more involved, and the hours were a great deal longer. He needed a break, even if the whole idea of it went against his workaholic grain. He needed to spend time with Sheree; his wife probably saw less of him than his work colleagues.

And then there was Trey. By the time the show's third season ended in 1993, he was six months old, already a veteran of television studios, but his father still needed time to know him better.

Relaxing as it was, idleness didn't come easily to Will. He'd been so used to being busy every day that it was hard to adjust to a rhythm of simply not doing anything. At least he could plan ahead for the next season of "Fresh Prince," and lay the groundwork for making some changes.

It was a little oasis in a life that had been filled with work for too long. In part, perhaps, Will felt he *had* to keep working, since the last time he'd let things slide, he'd ended up close to bankrupt. But the kid who'd let that happen didn't exist anymore. Will was making very good money— although not quite as good as he did in 1988—and he wasn't trying to spend it in any mad way. In fact, financially, he was very comfortable now.

One thing he and Sheree did over the summer was buy a house, but not up in the Hollywood Hills, or any of the traditional locales for stars. Instead, he stuck quite firmly to his suburban roots and moved out of Los Angeles, up to Thousand Oaks, where he lived on the same street as Bob Hope—hardly what anyone might expect for a former rap star.

It was an hour's commute to the studio each day, but it did offer a number of advantages. Real estate was significantly cheaper there, so he could buy much more for his dollar. In Will's case that meant an eight-thousand square-foot adobe style house, with a pool and grounds, including a one-hole golf course.

"Everyone complains about the distance," he admitted, "but you feel like you're away from L.A., and that's important."

And, indeed, short of being *very* rich, you'd have to be away from L.A. to afford something like that.

The trappings of his mansion in Philadelphia were also

a thing of the past. There were no cabinets full of cold cuts and a basketball hoop in the living room in Thousand Oaks. Will had grown up, he was a father. He still loved to play with the round ball, and even more to watch professionals playing, but golf was becoming his game—hence the small course in his backyard.

And the summer did at least give him a chance to get out and play, then come home to a place filled with art and African artifacts, wooden beamed ceilings, a stream (electronically controlled) running through the garden, tiled courtyards, and an atrium—virtually everything anyone could wish for. If Will ever needed to remind himself that he'd made it all the way back from the bottom to the top, this was his proof. About all it lacked was a recording studio, something he'd rectify in a few years, when he eventually returned to music.

Put simply, he had it all. It was a very comfortable life removed, both geographically and stylistically, from the hustle and bustle of Hollywood. His neighbors were more likely to be doctors and lawyers than actors, and he was accepted as just another member of an elite community—a secure, gated community, at that.

"In general," Will said, "the things I tend to like fit perfectly with the mainstream."

And during his time off, that was apparent from all the things he surrounded himself with. His family, his house, the occasional game of golf, grocery shopping. Will was middle America personified. The only exception was that his estate and his bank balance were a lot bigger than most.

But as he knew full well, "If I get comfortable, I get lazy," and the forces that kept driving him weren't about to let him get too relaxed. A few weeks off was one thing, but there was always that itch to return to work. He might not have had the title of busiest man in show business, but that didn't mean he wasn't casting faint, envious glances at it.

The day that pre-production began on the fourth season of "The Fresh Prince of Bel Air," he was there, on time, refreshed from his months of doing nothing, and ready to get to work. He was taking his new title of executive producer very seriously. It had been given to him as more than a sop (many shows—particularly sitcoms—have their stars as executive producers—but the level of involvement varies greatly), and he had to prove that he deserved it. With each year the show was becoming a little bit more of a challenge for him, as he admitted.

". . . Personally, I'm moving away from the character," he told *TV Guide*. "Will on the show doesn't have a wife and kid. I have to *act* now."

But act he could, finally. And back in the saddle, he seemed at ease.

"As long as I can do everything, I will. Quincy Jones said to me one time, 'You don't need to relax. You'll have all the time in the world to relax when you're dead.' "

And after a deliberate layoff, Will was trying hard to prove those words true. He was already talking about the next movie he was going to make, although what it would be remained to be seen. He and Sheree had discussed trying for a younger brother or sister to Trey. And to top it all off, he had nine months of very long days ahead of him with the series, showing the powers that be that they were right to promote him.

As he discovered, though, working for big changes was going to be a slower and more arduous task than he'd imagined. In fact, he'd be fighting every step of the way. Had he not been the star, it's unlikely he'd have altered the show as much as he did. But even then it stopped far short of the vision he had for it.

None of that stopped him pushing. But the reality was that "Fresh Prince" was a family show, and that was the way it would stay. The mold had already been set, and although Will saw the possibilities for it becoming something like a black version of "Roseanne," there was just no way on earth that NBC would allow that to happen. "The Fresh Prince of Bel Air" was what it was, family entertainment, with the emphasis on entertainment. The best Will could manage was to make some of the storylines more relevant, to reduce the farcical element in the show, and to make it less superficial.

Nor would the show rise to number one in the ratings under his leadership, although he'd been aiming for that since the beginning. In fact, during its six seasons it would never crack the top ten of primetime shows, even when it won its time slot. It was solid, regular viewing for many people across the country, without ever becoming the sort of stellar weekly event that "Seinfeld" or "Friends" would become.

In some ways that actually worked to the show's advantage. A little less was expected of it. There was slightly less pressure on both cast and crew to keep that top position. And that might have helped its longevity. Where most sitcoms seemed to create a rapid arc of rise and fall, "The Fresh Prince of Bel Air" just kept on going. By the end of the fourth season it had notched up ninety-nine episodes, one short of the magic hundred.

That number was magic in more ways than one. Not only did it give everyone a chance to celebrate, but one hundred shows made it eligible to put the previous seasons into syndication. And that, even more than the initial network showings, was where the money lay. It could be very lucrative for everyone concerned (indeed, the general feeling is that it's better to have a show that lasts long enough to be syndicated, rather than to be a star for one or two seasons), and "Fresh Prince" would be no exception.

But at the wrap party in spring 1994, that remained a few months away. The show had performed as well as ever, and Will's persistence had paid off in small ways, with some of the storylines, and the overall tone of the show. The characters were growing, in every way.

And so were the people who played them. Will was very definitely a man now, with his family. Even his son was growing in front of the rest of the cast, as he continued to visit frequently.

He was remarkably well-behaved in the studio, never throwing tantrums or expecting attention; it was as if he knew he couldn't be the center of this universe. He quickly realized that the red light (which came on for taping) meant something special, and would whisper "Sssh," to everyone around him, his finger on his lips.

That kind of behavior would continue. Once he began talking properly he would ask before taking something from the set to play with, and Sheree always seemed to be hovering in the background to supervise him as he watched his father at work.

For all that they seemed like the perfect family, though, it was only facade, the public face they displayed. As 1994 progressed, both Will and Sheree came to understand that their marriage simply wasn't working the way they'd hoped. A young child can place a strain on a relationship, but in this case it had nothing to do with Trey; quite the opposite. If anything, he was the glue holding them together.

Over the course of many long evenings at the house in Thousand Oaks, they tried to hash things out, to make it all work. It wasn't as if there was anger, or even bitterness. Things simply weren't working; they weren't happy as a couple. And no amount of words or talking was going to change that.

In its own way, it echoed the problems that Will Sr. and Caroline had undergone, as much as one couple's problems can recall another's. Certainly the last thing Will wanted was to separate, mostly for the sake of Trey. But he also knew that staying together could be more harmful to the boy in the long run.

There was no blame to be attached to either Will or Sheree. They'd married with their eyes open. Will might have been on the rebound when they met, and pursued her heavily, but she'd been the cool one who held him at bay for several months. When they'd fallen, they'd both fallen hard and fast.

Of course, by the very nature of Will's work, there were pressures that many people never experience. In public, going out for a meal, or even going to the grocery store, he could never be a completely private person; there would always be fans coming up, autographs to sign, while his wife remained off to the side. And then there was his work schedule. For nine months it was as if he was possessed by a television series, working long hours, five days a week. And no sooner had that pressure let up than he would plunge into a movie, which meant at least two more months of day-in, day-out slogging. There was no real time for himself, or his family. The fact that Will was, by nature, a workaholic, only seemed to make things worse.

The summer they'd spent together in 1993 had been wonderful, but it couldn't be repeated any time soon. In the end, they both concluded sadly, there was really no alternative but separation, followed by divorce.

At least, having lived through it with his own parents, Will had seen that it wasn't the end of the world, and it certainly wasn't the end of parental life. One thing that went beyond any doubt was that he loved his son, just as both his own parents had loved him, both before and after their divorce. Although he wouldn't have primary custody, there was no reason that he still couldn't be a real father to Trey. He was going to make sure he was, raising him with real, solid values that were far removed from Hollywood, to be a young man both he and Sheree could be proud of.

They realized that sharing custody of a young child meant that they'd have to be in frequent contact for quite a few years yet. So, even if they couldn't live together, they needed to be cordial, and in many ways present a united front, if they were going to raise their son right.

And it was also important that they didn't snipe against each other in public, either before or after the divorce. No axes would be ground in the media.

The most Will would ever say about it was that they'd married too young and too soon.

"When you don't know enough about yourself, you can't know someone else," he'd admit. And later, he'd be even more philosophical about things.

"You know how you're on the freeway and you see that one car on the side of the road? Thousands of cars drive by it. Well, every once in a while, it's your turn to be broken down. And you wait for the tow truck to come. That's how I view that time in my life."

It was a deft analogy, placing no blame; things just happened. And Sheree, too, was brief in her assessment of matters: "We were young, but we have a beautiful baby. Everything is cool—it worked out."

In many ways, things had been really brought to a head when Will's infant half-brother, Sterling, died in Philadelphia. Will Sr. had remarried and had another child. When the boy died of natural causes, it had an impact that reverberated through the entire Smith family, but most particularly with Will. He spent time with his father back in Philly, and the distance really gave him a chance to think about what was working in his life, and what wasn't.

And the marriage wasn't. Will and Sheree separated under amicable circumstances at the beginning of 1995, and quickly filed for divorce—better to have the legalities out of the way, for all concerned, to make the break clean and not linger, allowing them all to get on with their lives.

With Will's star status, it was impossible to keep matters out of the tabloids. But silence was one way to keep coverage to a minimum, at least until the divorce became final in December 1995, and the settlement was public knowledge. *Jet* published every last detail, down to the amount each paid their lawyer.

Indicating just how reasonable Will and Sheree had been with each other, much of the division of community property had already been made, "by mutual agreement." Will would keep the house, his production companies and businesses. Also his would be any syndication money from "The Fresh Prince of Bel Air," residuals from the airing of his movies on television, retirement and pension funds, all his copyrights, and the bank accounts that were in his name, as well as everything he'd bought before he married Sheree.

In turn, Will agreed to pay her $8,000 a month in child support until Trey was eighteen. He also had to establish an education trust, starting with $25,000, then adding $10,000 a year until 2010.

Sheree would receive $18,000 a month in spousal support, payable until she either remarried or died. Will had to establish a $1 million life insurance policy for Trey, and one for Sheree in the amount of $650,000 as security for future support.

On top of that, he agreed to give $250,000 towards the purchase of a new home for her, $900,000 cash, payable over four years, the 1992 Mercedes 120 they owned, $37,500 for her to purchase a new Mercedes S-320, and all the bank accounts in her name, or that she held jointly with someone other than Will.

As settlements went, it was an indication of how amicable things really had been. A few items, such as the money for a new Mercedes, might have seemed extravagant, but Will hadn't balked at any of it. Certainly, by Hollywood standards, he'd gotten off quite lightly. And he'd made sure that neither Sheree nor Trey would be lacking in creature comforts during their lives. He was, after all, in a position to afford to pay money like that without leaving himself broke. At the time of the divorce, just in the bank accounts, the couple had $1.2 million—hardly down to their last dollars.

The final part of the agreement covered custody of Trey. As Will and Sheree had agreed, she'd have primary custody, but Will was also going to be very involved, having the right to visit Trey "at all reasonable times and places." They'd already worked out a custody schedule for holidays.

Will might no longer be a husband, but he definitely wasn't about to turn his back on being a father.

CHAPTER SEVEN

THE summer of 1994 could almost be pinpointed as the time Will Smith began his ascent to superstardom. The season of "The Fresh Prince of Bel Air" had concluded quite successfully, Will's first at the helm. Even if he hadn't been able to do most of the things he wanted, he certainly hadn't disgraced himself. After taking the previous summer off, he knew he was ready to do another film. At home, things were slowly falling apart.

What he needed was something radically different. Not that *Six Degrees of Separation* hadn't been; but something that could be both funny and dramatic, that might stretch him in a few other directions as well as giving him some pleasure.

The opportunity to do all that in one package came with the script of *Bad Boys*. With the success of *Beverly Hills Cop* and *Lethal Weapon,* it was the kind of formula that could have big money written all over it, if the right actors could be found. In Will and Martin Lawrence, it seemed as if the producers had them. Will was already an established name, and Lawrence was one of the real up-and-coming comics. He'd started out in stand-up, before progressing to his own show, "Martin," on Fox. Along the way he'd also made a few movies, including the one Will had always cited as the first film of the hip-hop generation, *House Party.* Like Will, he was star material, but he was still waiting for the right vehicle to make himself properly known.

Actually, on paper *Bad Boys* seemed like a risky proposition. Would middle America pay to go and see an action-drama with two black cops? *Lethal Weapon* had spawned sequels, but that had Mel Gibson. *Beverly Hills Cop* had starred Eddie Murphy, who was already close to a household name when it arrived on screens.

The producers were willing to gamble that audiences would flock to see the movie. Especially with the twist that Lawrence, best known for playing the wild single man, would be married, a station wagon-driving parent. Will, associated with being the straight arrow, would be Mike Lowery, the bachelor who'd inherited a fortune, driving a Porsche and quite decidedly single.

Playing against type was one of the things that attracted Will to the film.

"My role in *Bad Boys* is completely different from anything I have ever done," he said. "[Mike Lowery] is a playboy and I have never been a playboy. On screen and in real life, I've always been the guy who couldn't get the girl. I like the change and I like the stretch. I went from 'Fresh Prince' to *Six Degrees* and back to 'Fresh Prince' and now to *Bad Boys*. I enjoy doing different things and trying to keep the audience off-balance. I really like that a lot."

So Will was in, and Lawrence had agreed to play the other cop, Marcus Burnett. Now the burning question was—would there be any electricity between them? Could they work well together? If not, things were going to be very difficult.

"When I met Will, there was an immediate chemistry between us," Lawrence said, "and I knew if we could get that chemistry on camera, we'd be cool. We opened our hearts to each other and decided we could be partners."

With that taken care of, things could begin to move along. For Will, that meant spending time with a trainer. He was tall, but he'd always been something of a beanpole, skinny. Now, to look like a cop, he needed to add muscle and definition.

"As much as it is a movie, it's real, too," he noted. "There is a lot of physical work that goes into it."

And that was no understatement. The movie's humor would come from Will and Lawrence, but there was going to be as much action as anything in *Lethal Weapon* or the *Die Hard* series.

The humor came not only from the characters themselves, and their relationship as partners, but from the fact they had to switch—Lawrence had to become Mike Lowery, and Will had to be Marcus—to keep hold of a witness to a murder. The murder was a crime that they needed to solve quickly in order to recover the $100 million of heroin that had been stolen from police headquarters. Of course, the witness was female and beautiful, the future Mrs. David Duchovny, Tea Leoni, a woman who seemed to be ninety percent leg.

Set in Miami, it inevitably had a flavor of "Miami Vice," a show that changed forever the way America looked at police series. And though the plot required some extreme suspension of disbelief at times—it's unlikely that cops who'd killed as many people as this pair would be allowed out on the street—the pairing of Will and Lawrence was as good as anything that had come along in the movies for a long time.

"I think the key to developing a good partnership is developing that mental link where you can just look at someone and know what's up," Will suggested. "It's Will and Martin, but it's a real action movie with some really good action sequences. Working with Martin was great. He's a comedic genius; in fact, he's a comedic geyser. We'd never worked together before, but it never felt like we were strangers—we got to really know each other. The chemistry was really great."

Although there was a script, once the two of them began working together, it seemed to largely get thrown out of the window. Director Michael Bay was content to let them play off each other; it worked, and it was definitely adding to the movie.

"We basically ad-libbed every scene," Will recalled. "It was two and a half months of two of the silliest guys in comedy doing exactly what they wanted to.''

Well, not always *exactly* what they wanted to. The action sequences—and there were plenty of them in the film—had to be very carefully choreographed, and there were times the actors had to do their own stunts.

That led to what Will called the Michael Bay encyclical. Will and his bodyguard, Ernest Anderson, came up with the encyclical.

''I said, 'Mike, that's fine, I'll do all of the stunts, but at any moment when my buddy here realizes I've been injured, he's been instructed to knock you out.' ''

The director never lost consciousness.

While he was in Miami, another role came up that Will really wanted, that of Bobby Earl in *Just Cause,* a thriller starring Sean Connery and Laurence Fishburne. It wasn't a major or even pivotal role, but there was plenty of drama—another challenge for Will. His name was big enough now, and he'd proved his acting credentials, to the point where he was at least interviewed.

''The producers and director said, 'We'll take a meeting, but we already know it's no. The role's too close to what you did in *Six Degrees of Separation.*' ''

In the intensity of the shoot, that was put aside. Miami in the early summer was hot and sticky, and the days of filming were long and gruelling, both mentally and physically. But Will and Lawrence were able to keep their verbal sparks flying off each other. And Bay had to ensure things moved along swiftly and smoothly; the budget was generous, but within that the action sequences were expensive. With so many things being destroyed each time, the first takes had to be perfect, most particularly at the climax, with cars, a garbage truck, and an airplane all exploding. America seemed to have an insatiable fascination with the destruction of objects, the more and bigger, the better, and *Bad Boys* intended to deliver.

By the time it was all wrapped, the producers knew they had a winner—if they could get people into the theaters to see it. That brought back the question that had been asked at the very beginning: Would the U.S. accept a black cop, buddy, action movie?

Obviously, for it to make money, the country had to, and advertising was the way to get customers to part with their money. The movie had no star names of the kind who would automatically draw people in large numbers, and that meant taking another tack, enticing them with both the camaraderie and the action.

That's exactly what they did. For weeks before *Bad Boys* opened on Memorial Day weekend, 1995, trailers played on television, Will and Lawrence driving along singing the "Cops" theme (a song known as *Bad Boys*), arguing, and things exploding.

It looked guaranteed to intrigue and excite, but the results wouldn't be known until the first weekend's grosses were announced. When that figure came out—$15.5 million—it was everything the backers could have hoped for, and more. From such a powerful beginning, the film could only climb.

And the reviews it began to receive in the press only helped it. While one called it "relentless formulaic fodder for the explosion-starved; it's loud, shallow, sexist, and a complete waste of time," most were far more generous to both the actors and the effects. "The climactic shootout inside an airplane hanger, complete with a 727 blowing sky-high slides the film into overdrive," commented *Rolling Stone*. "It's all special effects noise and nonsense. We're not fooled. Lawrence and Smith are the real firecrackers."

In the *Chicago Tribune*, Michael Wilmington didn't like the movie, but loved both Will and Lawrence. "These two are so good—at least potentially—it's maddening they have this kind of movie built around them." The praise for them together seemed unanimous. *Entertainment Weekly* felt, "There's a spark of canniness in casting Lawrence and Smith against type. Smith, the clean-cut sitcom prince, plays the swinging bachelor, and Lawrence, notorious for the raunchiness of his stand-up routines, is the devoted fam-

ily man. . . . Lawrence and Smith are winningly smooth
comic actors.''

They made an ideal screen team, but the one who
seemed truly larger than life, and more comfortable that
way, was Will. Before he'd been a rapper, a comic actor
who had his own TV series, and someone proving himself
as a film actor. Now he'd gone beyond any of that. He was,
quite simply, a star. Already a well-known quantity, this
was a movie that took him to another level. It made him
one of the biggest black stars in America, arguably more
recognizable than even Denzel Washington.

People was dazzled by him, noting that ''The unfailingly
ingratiating Smith glides through the movie . . . Smith is an
actor with a refined sense of comedy. He is also physically
imposing enough to pull off a serious action film.'' And
Entertainment Weekly singled him out, saying, ''Smith especially holds the camera with his matinee-idol sexiness
and his quicksilver delivery of lines. . . .''

This was something altogether different from anything
that had been written about Will in the past. Matinee-idol
sexiness? No one had thought of him as good-looking before, let alone in the matinee-idol class—which was far
more classic than ''hunk.'' And sexy? That, too, was a first
in print.

What *Bad Boys* did was change the perception of Will
Smith. Excellent as he was in *Six Degrees of Separation,*
that had been a serious film, more of an art film than anything else. It did what it was supposed to for Will, which
was to establish him as a serious actor. With that groundwork in place, he could move on from there, and *Bad Boys*
was a film that would take him to the masses. He really
acted the part of Mike Lowery, made him smooth and be-
lievable, with the comic edge. More than that, Will made
him irresistible.

The role vaulted him into another league. That was
partly due to the critics, but the bigger factor was the success of *Bad Boys* at the box office. The remarkable grosses
of the first weekend proved to be an indicator of what was

to come. By the time it left theaters, it had taken in $140 million domestically, and another $75 million abroad. And that was just in theaters, never mind the cable and video income which would acrue in the future.

With Hollywood's attention having changed from making films to the *business* of making films, the bottom line was king, and *Bad Boys* had a very impressive bottom line. Combined with his reviews, that was enough to put the star beside Will's name.

But long before the movie ever saw release, he was back in Burbank, on the set of ''The Fresh Prince of Bel Air'' for its fifth season.

The show had made him, he knew that, but he also realized he couldn't stay with it forever. He didn't *want* to stay with it forever, as he admitted to a reporter.

''Artistically, the show has made me feel somewhat crazed,'' he said, ''but I'll stick with it through the end of my contract.''

That meant two more years, and a total of six seasons. Coming back from his hiatus making movies was always difficult, particularly when it was something like *Bad Boys,* which kept the adrenaline flowing, to something where he had to be so tame. And the things he wanted to do as executive producer would rock the solid boat a little too much. He was definitely feeling the frustration.

''When I got into this business, the most important thing was to always try to stay on the edge. It's really difficult with television to be anywhere near the edge, especially Monday night at eight P.M.''

But the season began on a high note. On September 19, 1994, NBC aired the one-hundredth episode of ''Fresh Prince''—actually two half-hour episodes put together for a season opener under the title,''What's Will Got to Do with It.'' The show had lasted longer, and been far more successful, than most. It was cause for celebration, and the night it was transmitted, everyone did exactly that, at the House of Blues on Sunset in Los Angeles. Cast and crew brought spouses and partners, drinks flowed, speeches were made, sometimes full of exaggeration, none more so than Will's comment to reporters: "I want to do another hundred shows and make them as good as the first hundred!"

It was the heat of the moment, but Will wouldn't be around to reach episode two hundred, and he already knew it. In many ways, he couldn't have been timing his career better if he'd had a master plan. *Bad Boys* would come out at the end of the show's fifth season. He was already committed to make a film during the summer of 1995—one that looked as if it would make him into a megastar. Then he'd have one year left on his television contract. That would end as this other movie appeared, leaving him free to move smoothly into a film career.

It was masterful, even if did depend on the American public remaining avid fans of action and effects. But after so long, that seemed unlikely to change.

Just because Will had decided that his time on "The Fresh Prince of Bel Air" was finite, however, didn't mean he'd stopped caring about the show. As a workaholic, he was very attentive to details. There was no question of the quality slipping. After all, as both star and executive producer, his reputation was very much on the line.

But it was time for the Fresh Prince to do a little on-screen growing, which meant a serious girlfriend, Lisa, played by Nia Long. After all, the character had gone from high school to college. He was developing as a human being, and that meant some romance.

By now, of course, Will had become far removed from the "Will Smith" he was playing five days a week. In the beginning, the age difference—the fictional Will was some five years younger than his real-life counterpart—hadn't seemed too drastic, but now the life experiences had greatly diverged. It was time to start bringing them a little more into line.

Naturally, that didn't stop the show also being playful. "Will's Up the Dirt Road" brought in Jay Leno as a guest, when Will sold a false story about Leno to a magazine, and found himself sued by the host for $10 million. All that led to Will appearing on "The Tonight Show" to clear the air—a very suitable crossover, given that Will, in real life, was one of Leno's favorite and most frequent guests. And then there was "Will Is from Mars," which had Will and Lisa attending a surreal counseling session with Sherman Hemsley and Isabel Sanford reprising their roles as the Sanfords.

In fact, the continuing courtship of Will and Lisa provided the season's central theme. The other characters had their stories, but this was the backbone.

All in all, the season fulfilled a little more of what Will had hoped. He'd seen the Prince grow into a man. Although he hadn't addressed too many "issues"—the main one being the question of what was macho, in "Love Hurts"—there'd been enough for him to feel that his presence as executive producer had made a real difference.

But it wasn't enough for him to change his decision about renewing his contract. To be scrupulously fair, both to to the network and his colleagues, he gave his notice at the end of the season.

"I just felt it was time," he explained. "It was a discipline I needed to learn and I did. I will miss the characters and doing the show, but it was just time. Besides, I wanted to go out while the show was still hot. I never wanted to go out like a sucker, with them pushing me out."

His experiences in films were also making it harder to return to the same character year after year.

"I had done movies like *Six Degrees of Separation* and *Bad Boys,* I was up for more—including *Independence Day*—and the TV show just felt confining. You're pretty much one character, and there are not many peaks and valleys, just pretty much the same old, same old." And elsewhere he admitted that, "It became increasingly difficult to find that guy inside me. All the things 'Fresh Prince' stood for, all the fun he had, still exist inside me, it's just that those aren't the dominant aspects of my personality anymore."

It was a volatile time for Will. His decision to leave

"Fresh Prince" might have been final, but that didn't mean he was emotionless about it. Those involved with the show had become friends, almost like family in some ways. He was alone again, in the middle of a divorce, unable to be with his son all the time.

What he did have was more work, always the ideal thing for Will. If it couldn't make him forget his problems, it could at least fill his time to the point where he had very little time for introspection. And in *Independence Day* he was going to be very busy indeed.

CHAPTER EIGHT

INDEPENDENCE *Day* came about more or less by accident. Writer Roland Emmerich and producer Dean Devlin had made *Stargate* together, a science-fiction movie about parallel universes. It had done reasonably well at the box office, enough to ensure the pair would be listened to carefully when pitching any other projects.

At a press conference for *Stargate,* Emmerich was asked if he believed in other intelligences in the universe. He groped for an answer, finally saying no, then adding, according to Devlin,

"I believe in fantasy. I believe in the great 'What if?' What if tomorrow morning you walked out of your door and these enormous spaceships hovered over every single city in the world? What would you do? Wouldn't that be the most exciting day in the history of mankind? Of course, he then walked over to me and said, 'I think I've got our next movie.' "

Beyond any shadow of a doubt, it was a subject that fascinated people. "Star Trek," in all its incarnations, had been incredibly popular on television. "The X-Files" had become appointment viewing for a number of people.

Emmerich and Devlin went to Mexico, and in thirty days they'd come up with a script called "Independence Day." Arriving home, they sent it out at noon on a Thursday. By ten P.M. Friday it had been purchased by 20th Century Fox, and everything was go. As the next week began, so did pre-production.

But there was more to *Independence Day* than a shoot-'em-up sci-fi thriller.

"Roland and I are fans of the disaster films of the seventies," Devlin explained. "When we were writing *Independence Day,* we talked about the kinds of films we don't get to see any more and thought it would be great to revive that genre. The disaster films, of which Irwin Allen was the king, allowed us to see a wide group of characters that represented different aspects of the population. Because there was no single hero, the audience was never quite sure about the ending. The disaster films offered the audience an opportunity to enjoy a fulfilling, fun, popcorn kind of movie. An event film that was not totally predictable."

And that meant they needed a cast, if not of top names, then one powerful enough to carry their roles.

"The tradition of the disaster film, and even the World War II movies like *The Longest Day,* was to have strong actors," said Devlin. "Because the better the actor, the more the audiences get involved with the character and then they care about the adventure they go on. We really wanted to go for the best actors available and, fortunately, we have an exceptional cast."

"We tried to find the perfect actor for each part," Emmerich continued, "to assemble a cast that was balanced, because we wanted the audience to have the feeling that each character was equally important. So, in the face of disaster, it was possible that any of them could die and that losing any one of them would be a big loss. That obviously depended a lot on the actors we cast."

Essentially, the film revolved around three characters, President Thomas J. Whitmore, computer wizard David Levinson, and marine fighter pilot Captain Steven Hiller. Between them they formed the soul, brains, and heart of the film.

"Will Smith was clearly the heart of the movie," Devlin said, "the Everyman in America, the good GI Joe, like you would have seen in the old World War II movies. Bill Pullman's President, as the soul, was a man of honor who has to make some very tough decisions in dire circumstances and becomes a hero in the process. Jeff Goldblum, the brains, is so terrific at playing brilliant, quirky, endearing characters and I think he outdid himself in this.''

Will was the first choice of both Emmerich and Devlin to play Captain Hiller. Until *Bad Boys* appeared, however, the studio was a little more reticent, but with those numbers increasing every day, they were glad to have him on board. It wasn't on that performance, though, that the writer and producer had decided to cast him.

"We saw *Six Degrees of Separation*," Emmerich recalled, "and thought Will did a hell of a job there. He has this all-American quality about him. He's a guy's guy, but he's so charming and sure of himself that women like him.''

And Will himself knew it was a great part for him.

"The role was interesting, because it is definitely serious but the character is also funny. Before *Independence Day*, I usually played one or the other. I was also a big fan of the disaster films. I grew up watching them and it was fun to be in one. Captain Hiller is a regular guy, the kind of character I like to play, who finds himself in a very irregular situation. But he's definitely up to it.''

It brought together all the strands of Will's career into one character. From "The Fresh Prince of Bel Air," *Made in America,* and *Bad Boys,* he was able to draw on his comedy. From *Where The Day Takes You* and *Six Degrees of Separation* came the drama. And *Bad Boys,* again, brought in the action element, although by comparison it was crude. At this point Will couldn't have been offered a part that suited him more perfectly, or was more likely to advance his career, even though it was going to mean a long, tiring shoot.

By now he was used to the physical aspects of filming, which was why he prepared with a personal trainer. It made his body look more far more muscular—which a marine Captain certainly would—but it helped him reach a place, both mental and physical, where he was able to undergo the long, hot days.

It was a movie of two parts, really. There was the human element and the special effects, and the humans were probably easier to work with. Rarely had effects been employed on such a massive scale. As head of the model-making department, Mike Joyce noted, "After I read the script for the first time and we did a breakdown of the miniatures, I realized that there were more of them needed in this movie than probably any two movies combined. There were spaceships of all kinds, cities to build, aircraft, monuments . . . the whole gamut of just about everything you could do in movies."

There were three identical alien Destroyer craft, ranging from four feet in diameter to a massive thirty feet, a two-and-a-half-foot replica of the Lincoln Memorial, and the Statue of Liberty. In fact, one of the few models the team didn't have to construct was the White House. A scale version had been made for *The American President,* which was then used in *Nixon* before it was passed on to the *Independence Day* crew for what would prove to be a pyrotechnic end.

However spectacular the effects, in the end it would have to be the humans who carried the film and made people care about it. And for Will, that meant a lot of work, and a big responsibility.

"I was happy to be a black man saving the world in *Independence Day,*" he said. "Black people have been saving the world for years, and nobody knew it."

It was a flippant remark, but one which bore a kernel of truth. Most definitely, the film portrayed Will as a black role model.

"It makes you work harder," he admitted. "I want to play positive characters. I want to play characters that represent really strong, positive black images. So that's the thing I consider when I'm taking a role after I decide if it's something that I want to do. At this point, I don't want to play a gangster, unless it's a role that has a different or more positive message. It's a large part of why I don't rap now, because of the slant that rap music has taken.''

But there were plenty of everyday challenges in the filming. Acting against effects, rather than people, was a completely new experience for Will.

''If you're acting with an alien, it's a mark on the floor or something. . . . On the set, they'll say, 'Okay, look to the left and just say your line to the left,' and you're like, 'What the heck is that for?' But when you see it all together, it's amazing.''

It took a great deal of imagination on the part of the actors, and sometimes it became a little too much. When he and Goldblum were filming scenes flying inside the alien mothership, ''It was a riot. There were so many elements that weren't there. I'm sitting in a chair, someone yells, 'Explosion!' and I start jerking my body around like I'm having a severe back spasm. Meanwhile, I know I'm supposed to be looking at 12,000 aliens and their elaborate spaceship. A little voice inside me is saying, 'Will, you're sitting in a La-Z-Boy recliner losing your mind!'. . . . We just thought about the lunacy of it. Finally, I had to turn to Jeff and say, 'You know, man, if it was up to you and me to save the world, I think we better tell everybody just to surrender right now. It's over. We're toast.' ''

But that was hardly the most gruelling part of the shoot. That came with the locations filmed in Wendover, a small town on the border of Utah and Nevada, by the Bonneville Salt Flats.

It wasn't the most pleasant place on earth. The salt would eat into equipment, there were high winds and salt storms, and the summer temperature in the sun was one hundred and twenty-six degrees Fahrenheit.

In one scene, Will's character had to haul an alien in a sack across the salt flats. He'd shot him down in a dogfight and now he was taking him back to ''Area 51'' to be studied. As he dragged the bag, Will's language went far beyond the script—amusing the rest of the cast and crew, who'd gathered to watch.

As he'd done on the set in other films, Will took on the role of entertainer, the class clown he'd never quite managed to leave behind. And he was joined by Goldblum. On another occasion, while a Steadicam was being tediously set up on a dolly, the two of them began singing and dancing.

It seemed ridiculous, but it was one way of breaking up the boredom, and steadying the nerves that jangled in the heat.

"During those really hot, long days in the Wendover Salt Flats, his energy and enthusiam never failed," remarked Dean Devlin. "In fact, one day the sun just got to little Ross Bagley, who was only six and played Dylan. Will sat with him and talked to him, and pretty soon Ross felt better and wanted to go back out and shoot."

Having young Ross, who played his little cousin Nicky on "The Fresh Prince of Bel Air" around made it almost like old home week. Curiously, neither knew the other had been cast.

"I didn't know Will was in the movie until I saw him in the room getting fitted," Bagley recalled. "I said, 'I can't believe it.' "

It gave him a chance to see how the star of the show worked on the big screen, which was slightly different to his methods in Burbank.

"On 'Fresh Prince' Will was real silly," Bagley observed. "On *Independence Day* he was more serious but still fun. I had a whole lot of fun doing the movie."

And that wasn't the end of the connections. Vivica Fox, who played Will's love interest in the film—and Dylan's mother—had also been on "Fresh Prince."

"I did a 'Fresh Prince' episode five years ago," she recalled. "Will was crazy then, and he's crazy now. People love Will Smith. He's a really good person."

After the shooting was finished, there were still months of work to be done before the movie would be ready to be shown to anyone, even its cast. Actors and effects had to be merged. It was a long process, labor-intensive, and expensive. When everything was finished, it had cost $70 million to make. It had some five hundred computer-generated shots, on top of three-and-half-months of principal photography, and *ten* months of second-unit work.

But finally the people who'd put in all the effort had the opportunity to view the finished product—something of a necessity since they'd be the ones going out and publicizing it. *Independence Day*, or "ID4" as it became known (in the film the action begins on July 4), was going to be big, there was no doubt of that. The buzz was already out in the industry. The only question was exactly how big.

Even Will was amazed after seeing it.

"Thrills, chills, spills," he announced. "You'll laugh, you'll cry. You never know who's gonna die. This is a disaster film in the classic sense, in the tradition of *The Poseidon Adventure* and films like that. There's a threat that the planet is going to be destroyed and the aliens actually begin destroying it. It's warm, funny, it's chilling, all at the same time."

If it sounded like ad copy, it was merely because he was blown away by the finished product, as everyone involved with the movie was. It had no pretensions to high art. Like a more grounded version of *Star Wars*, it was an "us against them" theme, with us—Earth—as the underdogs. In a western it would have been the cavalry that saved the day; here it was a marine pilot and a computer genius not too strong on social skills. The good guys won in the end, thanks to American courage and ingenuity. It flew the stars and stripes quite strongly. It contained all the elements that make a film successful.

The release date was set, appropriately enough, for the July 4 weekend of 1996. It was up against some strong competition: *Twister, Mission: Impossible,* and *The Rock* all had elaborate effects of their own, and plenty of big names—Helen Hunt, Tom Cruise, and Nicholas Cage with Sean Connery, respectively. To go up against those—particulary the much-touted *Mission: Impossible*—was putting things very much on the line, although an elaborate ad campaign, which played heavily on the Fourth of July element, helped prepare people for a blockbuster.

And from the moment it opened, blockbuster was exactly what it was. Over its first weekend, the July 4 holiday, it took in $83.5 million, and within its opening week had passed $100 million in receipts, a new box-office record. Two months later it was close to $300 million in America alone.

"The Monday the first box-office numbers were announced," Will remembered, "my father woke me by calling me from Philadelphia at nine A.M., which made it six A.M. in L.A.. He'd just seen the numbers and said, 'Boy, you remember when I told you that if you work hard and focus you can have anything you want?' I said, 'Yeah, Dad, I remember.' He said, 'That's [crazy], boy. You're the luckiest [person] I ever met in my life.' "

It wasn't just the public that loved the film. For once, the majority of reviewers agreed with them. In *Newsweek*, David Ansen pointed out that "... if I were a 10-year-old boy, I'd probably think it was the coolest movie going," and Brian D. Johnson, writing in *Maclean's*, a Canadian magazine, called it "good fun—for those who don't mind their popcorn thrills spiked with a megaton dose of star-spangled jingoism." Lisa Schwarzbaum, in *Entertainment Weekly*, raved that "This rootin'-tootin' blockbuster is . . . adorable. It's as happily techno-horny as any chapter of the *Star Wars* trilogy . . . as corny as Kansas, high as the flag on the Fourth of July. And if you'll excuse the expression I use, it's intrinsically American fun." Only *People* cast a sour note, feeling that it was "*The War of the Worlds* with a *Poseidon Adventure* sensibility—a big, mechanical enterprise with a dried pea of a brain rattling around in the hull."

Will came in for his share of praise in the enterprise. He was "charismatic," "fabulously likable . . . the winningest former rapper and TV sitcom star ever to grab a $70 million production and make it his own," and "a swaggering cowboy dying to kick some alien butt."

It had tapped into a zeitgeist, the increasing national obsession with aliens, UFOs, and what might be "out there." It was the right film at the right time, and it landed Will on the cover of *Newsweek* on its July 8 issue.

But an adventure movie is at heart an adventure movie. There are good guys and bad guys, and people want to see the suspense, with the good guys winning in the end. In this case the package came wrapped in some extravagant effects. But it delivered the goods. It gave people what they wanted to see.

Not only in America, but throughout the world. It took off like no other film before it, breaking opening records in France and Britain when it was finally released there. By October 1996, when it finally left American theaters, it had brought in more than $318 million domestically, and another $174 million overseas. In the blockbuster contest, it was the year's undisputed winner.

Bad Boys had made Will a star; *Independence Day* transformed him overnight into a international name. Some two hours of movie time did more than the past six years put together, a statement on American popular culture.

"The day before *Independence Day* opened, people on the street were like, 'Will, what's up?' The day after, it was 'Hey, Mr. Smith, how are you?' There's a whole different level of respect."

Far more than ever before, he was now a public figure. His face had been recognized from television, obviously, but a movie star was larger than life. And while most of the time that meant respect and adulation, there were inevitably people—usually men—who thought he *was* Steven Hiller, tough and cocky, and wanted to fight him.

But the shoot was complete a year before the movie appeared, and Will had twelve months to go before the huge wave of adulation broke. In that time there was plenty of work to do, the final season of "The Fresh Prince of Bel Air." Knowing this would be the last, there was a slight air of sadness about the proceedings, but also a determination to make it the best yet, to go out on the highest possible note.

But something else happened in Will's life during the fall of 1995. For several years he'd been friends with actress Jada Pinkett, ever since the first season of "Fresh Prince," when she auditioned to play his girlfriend. At five feet tall she was considered too short to work with Will's six foot two, but the two formed a friendship, and saw each other socially.

With his marriage gone, and wanting to know exactly where it had gone wrong, uncertain about his emotional future, Will turned to his friends. Jada, or "Miss Jada" as he always referred to her, was among them. She'd just had a relationship collapse, too, with basketball player Grant Hill.

"I helped him understand what happened in his marriage," she said, "and he helped me see what happened in my relationship. He's become my best friend. There's nothing I can't say to him, nothing I can't share."

Neither was looking for romance, which was perhaps exactly why they found it with each other. And both were decidedly cautious about love on the rebound. Will had discovered the dangers of that already, when he began dating Sheree after Tanya Moore. But there was absolutely no denying the feelings they were discovering for one another.

Jada Pinkett was born in Baltimore, Maryland, on September 18, 1971. Her first name had come from a character on a soap opera, "The Secret Storm," that her mother watched every day.

But she was barely an infant when her mother, a nurse, and her father, a contractor, split up. It was her mother who raised her, with help from the extended family. In particular, her grandmother played an important role, helping bring out Jada's forthrightness.

"My grandmother was a social worker. At a very early age she taught me about the birds and the bees, about masturbation, about everything. I brought books home from school and she sat me right down and put it all on the table.''

Her teenage years were full of rebellion and experimentation, by her own admission, ''out of control.'' Boyfriends, sex, motorcycle accidents, even hair color.

''I've had every color,'' she admitted, ''blonde, blue, purple, fuchsia, red, black, sandy brown—everything.''

She was lucky, though, in attending a school where freedom of expression was encouraged—Baltimore School of the Arts—and there one of her best friends was the late rapper Tupac Shakur.

''He was really tight with my boyfriend,'' Jada recalled, ''so weekends we'd hang out. If he got into trouble with his mom, he'd come spend the night at my house, something like that.''

They both knew they were going to get out of town, and become stars. But for Jada, that route included college.

''I was a very bad student. My high school diploma was really a gift. I got into North Carolina School of the Arts and everybody was so happy they basically allowed me to graduate.''

College proved to be a grounding experience for her, although she didn't stay long. There was the lure of the big time, and that could only mean Los Angeles.

After the usual round of fruitless auditions, she finally landed in front of producer Debbie Allen, who was casting the sitcom ''A Different World.'' Jada read for her, and ''Debbie looked at me and she said, 'Sweetheart, you got angels on your shoulders,' and I was like, 'Whoa, she's right, I *do* have angels on my shoulders.' ''

The characters in the show were a distinct contrast to her own wild schooldays.

''We all worked very hard to give the show substance,'' she said. ''Too many kids spend more time watching TV instead of reading books. 'A Different World' was a program that not only took place in an educational environment, but where the characters were young people who carted about their futures. Hopefully, we served as good role models.''

Inevitably, she met Will. They were both part of the young black group working in television; they had mutual friends and interests. But their paths didn't cross often—both Will and Jada were busy.

A couple of years after starting in television, she had her first film under her belt, *Menace II Society,* It was a very bleak, but completely realistic, portrait of life in South Central Los Angeles, full of violence, but without ever using it exploitatively. Directed by twenty-one-year-old twins, Albert and Allen Hughes, it was acclaimed by critics, and won two awards.

As debuts went, Jada's was small, but she couldn't have picked a better film for beginning her movie career. She capitalized on it quickly, making four movies in succession, *The Inkwell, Jason's Lyric, Tales From The Crypt Presents Demon Knight,* and *A Low Down Dirty Shame.*

The Inkwell had its moments, but instead of an edge it veered on the side of the sentimental. *Jason's Lyric,* set in Houston, featured Jada as a waitress caught between two brothers, and also showed her first—and last—love scenes on camera. *Demon Knight* was nothing more than a full-length version of the popular television show. *A Low Down Dirty Shame,* however, revealed a different side of Jada. It teamed her with writer/director/actor Keenan Ivory Wayans, one of the first people she'd met after traveling west. He played a private detective, and she was his secretary, Peaches, always making wisecracks and saving the day. It was all spoof, and though it wasn't entirely successful, Jada's performance brought her to the attention of a wider public.

Part of that wider public was a friend of Will's—Eddie Murphy. Since 1992's *Boomerang,* his movie career had been skidding downhill. *Beverly Hills Cop 3, The Distinguished Gentleman,* and *Vampire In Brooklyn* had all pretty much sunk without a trace. He was happy, married, living not in Los Angeles, but on a farm in New York with his wife and children. But he wanted a good comeback film. And in a remake of Jerry Lewis's 1963 hit, *The Nutty Professor,* it looked as if he might have found it. For once he wasn't controlling everything, just concentrating on what he did best—being funny. His Professor Sherman Klump was even better than the original, thanks in part to the special effects available. It also brought Jada to the forefront, giving her the female lead (played by Stella Stevens in 1963), and when the film became successful, it brought her a good measure of fame.

Ironically, she almost didn't make it, since she'd been approached to do another film at the time.

"They wanted me to do *Independence Day,*" she said, "and I couldn't do it because of *The Nutty Professor,* but we really had to sit and think about that."

And then came her relationship with Will.

"It took me by surprise," she admitted. "To me, Will just used to be a goofy, lanky, plays-too-much guy. He used to get on my nerves. Then we went to dinner one night and I saw something totally different in him. He was stressed about his marriage and he was talking about all these different things, and I was, like, 'He's a man now. He's got a kid. He's been married. He's actually grown up.' It grew from there, slowly but surely."

More than Will, Jada was a realist, as he quickly came to learn.

"Jada is the first person I've been with willing to accept that it's not always going to be great, but that's okay."

As had happened to Will in the past, the relationship quickly seemed to move beyond friendship, once it had ignited. It gave a steadiness to his life that he enjoyed, and that he also seemed to need. Will was no less of a workaholic than he had been, but he appeared far more comfortable with a solid emotional base behind him, and Jada could offer that. In the same business, with many of the same experiences (more, in fact; she'd even worked behind the camera, directing the video for Gerald Levert's "How Many Times"), she could understand and sympathize with the pressues Will faced every day, and actively help him with them.

For the moment, there was no question of her moving into the house at Thousand Oaks. She had her own life, her own place, a condo in L.A., and that was the way she liked it. All of a sudden Will was an important part of her, but she still had plenty to do on her own, and that included a new movie, *Set It Off,* which would team her with Queen Latifah and Blair Underwood.

"It's about four L.A. women who are dealing with oppression in one form or another. They make a bad decision to get out of the squeezes they're in—which is to rob banks. It's basically *Thelma and Louise Wait to Exhale.* I was happy to be part of a movie that was about us as women. They're always talking about what the black man has to go through and his struggles and you never see our side of the story."

The one thing Jada didn't do in *Set It Off* was appear naked. For the scene that required it, she used a body double, in part because she hadn't been pleased with the way the love scenes in *Jasons's Lyric* turned out, but "Also, now I'm in a relationship."

With the completion of *Independence Day,* and only one more season of "The Fresh Prince of Bel Air" Will was a hot property. The word was already goping around that the film was going to be huge, and it was obvious that Will was setting his sights quite firmly on a major movie career.

But one thing he hadn't expected, in the fall of 1995, was a phone call from one of the major players in the industry.

"Steven Spielberg called me at home," he said, "and I was sitting around in my underwear—that just didn't feel right, talking to him while I was in my underwear, so I got changed—and then he sent a helicopter to bring me out to his home in East Hampton. I flew out there, and sat down and talked with him, and found out that Tommy Lee Jones was involved as well as Barry [Sonnenfeld, director] and Steven—*I* call him Steven—and [Industrial Light and

Magic] were doing the special effects, with Rick Baker do-ing the make-up effects. So, of course, I was in.''

More to the point, ''Steven just said, 'You have to do this movie. We don't even want to talk about it.' . . . You can't say no to Steven Spielberg.'' So in October, Will signed a contract with Columbia for $5 million—quite firmly in the star range—that committed him to be one of the stars of *Men in Black,* which would film the following summer.

Before he could think about that, he had plenty of re-sponsibilities to consider in Burbank. Knowing it would be the final season, the writers would be able to round things off, to give the series closure. They'd leave on the highest note, with, eventually, 149 shows to their credit.

For the others in the cast, making the break might have been harder than for Will. He, after all, was moving on of his own volition. They hadn't vaulted into the superstar class the way he had. But they were still magnanimous, as Alfonso Ribiero summed up: ''So much in Will's life has changed, and it changed him. But his TV role stayed the same. . . . It's been great to have him as a brother and a friend for all these years.''

The finale came in March 1996, when the final episode (to be broadcast May 20) was taped. Everything was rounded out, with no loose ends left. Hilary and Ashley had already decided to move to New York, and after that Uncle Phil and Aunt Viv decided to sell their house and follow them to the East Coast, with Carlton and Nicky going along. Even Geoffrey, the butler, was leaving, returning to England. And that would leave only Will, the transplant, out in Los Angeles, finishing college there.

As they had done before, the writers brought in stars of older black sitcoms. In this case it was ''The Jeffersons'' (again) and ''Diff'rent Strokes,'' where members of the families came to view the Banks' residence when it was put up for sale.

When the film stopped running, and the audience had left the taping, it was all over, for the very last time. The evening had been filled with emotion, but it wasn't complete yet. There was still the annual wrap party, this one particularly memorable.

". . . I think I spent ten or fifteen minutes crying my eyes out," Tatyana Ali said, "like everybody else in the cast, because it was all over."

Cast and crew, everyone was given a moment in the limelight, to speak and share memories of the show and the people.

"The audience related the character to reality," Will said when he stood up to speak. "When I said a line, the audience didn't feel I was acting. What that allowed me as an artist was to more effectively carry my audience wherever I wanted them to go."

And looking around at the faces gave Will a chance to consider just how far he'd come in such a short time. From not being able to act at all during the first shows, he'd broken out in an unimaginable way.

But even more than being a vehicle for Will, Tatyana Ali observed, the show had done a great service to teenagers.

"From the fan mail I've received, I know the show has helped many teens get through difficult situations in their lives. We've touched on real problems kids have—drug use, sex, prejudices, inner-city problems. Even if we couldn't offer them solutions, our show has shown them that they are not alone."

With that, and six years of entertainment, the curtain fell. At least, in a way. The show continued, and continues still, in endless re-runs, syndicated to stations across the U.S. and throughout the world. Every day it's seen somewhere, in some places several times a day. And that means, no matter what else he does, Will will never be able to completely escape the Fresh Prince in his past.

And although he'd put it behind him, the Prince's legacy was nothing to be ashamed of. Both as a rapper and as a comic actor, the persona had given hours of pleasure to literally millions of people. With Jeff, he'd made what were really landmark recordings in hip-hop, helping to bring it into the mainstream of American music, where it now occupied center stage. In many ways, without the initial success of a Jazzy Jeff and a Fresh Prince, the way might never have been clear for the big Puff Daddy hits of 1997, which, like Will's tracks, were essentially pop music. In television, his show had largely taken up the torch of ''The Cosby Show.'' It never traded on stereotypes, but celebrated the black middle class; fully acknowledging their existence, providing role models, and making its points without ever being heavy-handed or didactic.

The Fresh Prince, both show and person, had been Will in transition from adolescent to man, showing himself to the world, growing right in front of his audiences. From rapper to TV star to movie idol was a steep progression, but he'd managed it smoothly and intelligently. At first, on television, it seemed he might have taken on too much, trying to run before he could walk. But in his quest to be the best at everything he did, he'd learned quickly and proved he really could cut it. In the movies he'd moved more slowly, taking in the craft, going in stages, but always stretching himself, until it was time to bloom.

And now it was time to retire the Prince. He'd served his purpose, but at twenty-seven Will was definitely a man, a parent, and divorced, with a tremendous film career ahead of him. The Fresh Prince had associations that plain Will Smith didn't. Will had made the jump the Prince, however good he was, would never be capable of. Will had become the star the Prince always hoped to be. And even bigger stardom was ahead.

CHAPTER NINE

ONE thing Will had decidedly never wanted was to be pigeonholed, but now he was making his second science fiction film in a row. And he was saving the world for the second time in a row, quite an awesome responsibility for someone who was still a few years short of thirty.

Of course, the two movies had virtually nothing in common, besides featuring aliens. Where *Independence Day* was quite deliberately an edge-of-the-seat ride, *Men in Black*, as the new film was to be called, was pure comedy.

The story's genesis was in a none-too-successful comic book, surprisingly. Written by Larry Cunningham, the series of six, which appeared in the late eighties, inspired by a rash of UFO sightings in his home state of Tennessee, it seemed to vanish into the vortex.

However, at least someone in Hollywood had been reading them, and in 1992, producers Walter Parkes and Laurie MacDonald bought the rights, on behalf on Steven Spielberg's production company, Amblin. Initially, there was plenty of talk about Spielberg himself directing the project.

"What we liked about the comic book was that it kind of posited the idea that there were these 1500 or so aliens living among us that needed to be policed," Parkes said. "Since no one [from other worlds] chooses to live on Earth, it attracts low-life scum from around the universe, and that's why you need guys like the Men in Black to shake them up."

The idea was interesting, but it lay in limbo for a long time.

"The script had been around for years," said director Barry Sonnenfeld in 1997. "But these alien movies are hard to figure out. I was sent this script about four and a half years ago, and I liked it very much because it seemed so different. While we were trying to figure out if we were going to make this movie or not I was also trying to get *Get Shorty* off the ground at another studio.

"Eventually MGM agreed to make *Get Shorty,* so I moved off *Men in Black,* they hired another director, they fired another director, I finished *Get Shorty,* and then ran into Barry Josephson—the head of production at Columbia—at a restaurant in Los Angeles. I went up and told him that I would be finished on *Get Shorty* in six months and if he was prepared to wait I would love to do the movie with Tommy Lee Jones and Will Smith."

Prior to *Get Shorty,* Sonnenfeld had directed the wildly successful *Addams Family, Addams Family Values,* and the far less memorable *For Love Or Money.* He'd started out as a cinematographer, and still wasn't a "big" name.

Nowhere near as big as Tommy Lee Jones, anyway. In fact, Jones was the first one firmly signed to the film, although he was reportedly less than happy with the original script. But he was mollified by both a $2 million pay raise, and the fact that Spielberg himself signed on as the executive producer. He was set to play Kay, but they still needed a Jay, the other lead. This was before the release of *Independence Day,* when Will Smith became a part of America's consciousness.

"They signed [Jones] straight away," Sonnenfeld recalled, "but of course since the number one and number two movies on that day did not star Will, I had to wade through people like Keanu Reeves and Chris O'Donnell and convince them that they didn't want to be in the movie. Then I had to wait around for Will."

And that, of course, where where Spielberg used his clout, simply telling Will that this was a movie he had to be part of. And who was Will Smith to turn down the most successful person in cinematic history?

Once the two leads had been settled, Sonnenfeld quickly found his main supporting character, the New York City pathologist whose memories of alien corpses were always being erased. He wanted, and signed, Linda Fiorentino, whose biggest credit has been as the extremely sexy woman in *The Last Seduction*.

"Barry Sonnenfeld just asked me to do it," she explained. "I loved his stuff and I wasn't working, so I said, 'Yes.' I don't put a whole lot of thought into it like other people do. I kind of make snap decisions on what's offered to me."

With all that in place, Sonnenfeld was ready to move on. But long before shooting could begin, there was the gigantic matter of special effects. By its very nature, *Men In Black* would need a lot of them, far more, even, than *Independence Day*. There would be aliens of all shapes and sizes. That meant a lot of work on the part of Industrial Light and Magic, which supervised all the effects, and Rick Baker's Cinovations, which designed and built all the aliens.

And, of course, it meant that once again Will would be acting with aliens, which he was beginning to see as standard operating procedure now.

But no matter how scintillating all the effects and computer-generated shots, this film, like any other, depended upon its actors and its script. It was, after all, a comedy, and that meant it had better be funny or the audiences would be staying away in droves.

The concept itself had great potential; as producer Parkes said, "there's something inherently funny about the situation of the classic tough guy cops getting heavy with the guys they're policing—because the guys are aliens. . . . The MIB just go about their business, paying no attention to that bizarre fact. It calls for a certain deadpan attitude . . . Barry is a comic director who doesn't rely on jokes. He relies on understanding the comic situation and playing it absolutely straight."

And that, really, was the crux. It was played very

straight, and the juxtaposition of the normal and the absurd made for the humor. No one, really, could play it any straighter than Tommy Lee Jones. He'd played it way over the top as Harvey "Two-Face" Dent in *Batman Forever,* but his reputation was that he was like granite.

"The great thing about Tommy is that he doesn't know he's funny," observed Sonnenfeld. ". . . He suffers no fools, but all he ever wants is direction."

And a script, which, in the initial stages, was very unfocused.

"The problem was that the screenplay, though a great idea, took place everywhere but in New York," Sonnenfeld said. "So I told the producers, 'My feeling's that if the aliens exist, they're in New York.' I grew up there, I live outside New York, and aliens would feel so comfortable there. Most wouldn't even have to wear a disguise! They could all get jobs driving cabs."

It seemed so obvious, but once they'd settled on that focus, everything became clear—although, according to Jones's character Kay, there were actually far fewer alien cab drivers than might have been expected. It was a case of putting a slight twist on the real to make it surreal—as in the supermarket tabloids, which became superb investigative journalism about aliens on earth.

Will played a New York City cop who'd caught a particularly speedy alien—and on foot, at that—only to have Agent Kay of the Men in Black, a super-secret division of the Immigration and Naturalization Service, erase his memory of the event with the handy neuralyzer. After that he was summoned for testing, along with the best and brightest from every branch of the services, to possibly fill a vacancy among the MIB. On Kay's insistence, he was chosen, and found himself plunged into a life very different from what he'd known before.

The first thing was the anonymous uniform, black suit and shoes, white shirt, black tie.

"The difference between you and me?" Will, now known as Jay, said to Kay. "I make this look good."

Once Will hit the set, he was himself, undaunted by the dour reputation of Tommy Lee Jones, or the invisible, but towering, presence of Spielberg behind the scenes.

"Will on the set is incredibly relaxed, self-confident and at ease with himself," Sonnenfeld said. "He's always energetic, bouncing on his toes, and, usually, punching my arm. He's just got too much energy. And because as the director I was usually the nearest guy to him, whenever I was talking to him or directing him he'd just be shadow-boxing with me. Except he was actually hitting me. And he's huge! He's really strong. So I'd go home every night with bruises on my left shoulder."

Notably, though, Will didn't try to get physical with Jones, who'd played football for Harvard.

"He's kind of really quiet and strong-looking, so you make yourself uncomfortable," Will recalled. "Also, his sense of humor is so different. People don't know how to take it. Personally, I enjoy every word that comes out of his mouth. He's a riot." Once they were used to each other, Will added, "We had a ball. A couple of divorced guys just hanging out."

The whole set took on aspects of insanity at times. One afternoon, Sonnenfeld, who was supposedly in charge, stopped the shoot to announce that he was the best shoe-kicker in America, announcing he could hit any target within thirty yeards.

For the next forty-five minutes he attempted to kick his shoe into a trash can an assistant had placed, fully thirty yards away. He never even came within ten yards of the can. But Sonnenfeld continued to insist he was the best shoe-kicker in America.

That was when Tommy Lee Jones arrived on the set, and Will decided to have some fun of his own.

"Barry, Tommy could probably beat you," he said.

"Tommy Lee wouldn't even feel comfortable taking his shoes off in front of people," Sonnenfeld replied.

The challenge was on. Without a word, Jones lined up, yards from the trash can.

"Then he takes his shoe off and from about forty yards sinks it right in the trash can," Will recalled in amazement. "It doesn't look like he's even given it any energy. It doesn't look like he's even paying attention. He just took his shoe off, kicked it, sunk it in the trash can and went and sat down. It was like, 'Somebody grab that shoe for me, please.'"

But that type of madness and laughter was quite typical of what went on during the making of *Men in Black,* much of it instigated by Sonnenfeld himself, who proved to be a very funny man.

"He's *deeply* funny, that boy," Linda Fiorentino agreed. "That's basically what we did on the set; we laughed at Barry. Will and I would laugh at Barry all day long, and we always knew our scenes were working because he would be behind the camera laughing."

Sonnenfeld even tickled Jones's funnybone.

"Nobody has ever made me laugh like Barry Sonnenfeld. In his direction he kept telling me, 'Tommy, do it flatter.' The result is really deadpan. From what I've seen, it's really hysterical. If you're going to do comedy, you should do it with the best. And Will and Barry are the funniest people in the business."

Jones even played up his curmudgeonly side to humorous effect, according to Sonnenfeld: "Tommy would say, without fail, 'The words suck, the writer didn't know what he was doing, what he meant, why this scene exists at all. It's overwritten and it doesn't make sense and it's not funny but hey, I'm getting too much money to complain. So tell me where to stand, what to say, and I'm there for you.'"

However, when it came to film the stunts, things changed a little. Some things, like Will being tied to bungee cords and thrown fifty feet through the air into a pile of foam pads demanded the resurrection of the Michael Bey encyclical, as Sonnenfeld learned. But even there, the director negotiated a compromise, according to Will, saying, "Okay, listen, how 'bout if you do get hurt I don't have to get knocked out right now. Maybe later when

I'm not looking. I think it would hurt a lot less."

In the end Will did the stunt, and catapulted across the set. Sonnenfeld asked, "Am I okay?"

Will stood up and grinned. "You're fine."

Some of the location shooting was on the streets of New York, and it was there that Will had his first taste of what it meant to be a film star, and it wasn't necessarily something that made him feel loved. A woman driving along saw him, and was so distracted that she drove straight into another car. Instead of taking care of the accident, she ran straight over to Will and asked for an autograph.

It was an indication of the change that *Independence Day* had effected, and one, he realized, that would become even greater when *Men in Black* finally reached theaters. To him, the film seemed like it could be a real cinematic landmark, which made him especially happy to be a part of it.

"This is the type of movie that will mark points in people's lives," he said. "I remember the day *Star Wars* came out. That's the kind of movie *Men in Black* is. *Men In Black* is going to inspire the next Steven Spielberg, who is still nine years old. It's going to inspire people to take it to the next level. There's digital work in this movie that you've just never seen anything like before."

This was the Will who wanted to be the best, and if possible, the first. As in everything he undertook, it brought out his competitive side, even if he was only competing against himself.

But one thing he'd never done, and had never had any desire to do, was carry a film alone. In all the movies he'd made, he was part of a team onscreen. A featured player, and often the most memorable, but never—with the possible exception of *Six Degreees of Separation*—in a position where things relied solely on him. And the actors he'd worked with had been of very high quality, whether it was Whoopi Goldberg in *Made in America,* Donald Sutherland in *Six Degrees of Separation,* Martin Lawrence in *Bad Boys,* Jeff Goldblum in *Independence Day,* or now Tommy

Lee Jones. Will understood innately how he came across best.

"My whole concept of making movies is to *never* carry them alone. I want to always work with the best actors . . . as well as the best directors and producers. I'm not self-indulgent in that way, I just want to make great movies."

And he also knew that for all the disconcerting adulation he might be receiving, he still wasn't an above-the-titles star. In fact, in *Men in Black* he'd receive second billing to Jones. But true stardom was just really just around the corner. With *Independence Day* he'd truly graduated to the A-list.

"Before *Men in Black*," he mused, "I wasn't the first or second or thirty-eighth choice for this type of movie. I'm getting more calls from people who have faith in my abilities. It just makes you feel good that big studios are willing to bank on you for their big movie of the summer."

He was right to say that, because the film was scheduled to be released on the July 4th weekend, 1997, giving Will two Julys in a row when he'd be saving the world.

"Oh yeah, July 4th is Big Willie weekend now. But that's a good thing, to be linked to new movies. In choosing the films that I want to do, the big fourth of July block-buster is exciting and it's really tempting to keep making those blockbusters, but I want to try other things and do different types of movies too."

But there were still a few bumpy rides before that could happen, not the least of which was the ride Jay and Kay took through the tunnel, where their standard issue Ford LTD was transformed at the push of a button, into a su-percar that drove along the roof. It was a remarkable mix of live action and computer graphics, some of the digital work that had impressed Will so much.

"Before we could shoot the computer-generated footage of the 'supercar' going through the tunnel," explained vi-sual effects director Erci Brevig, "we needed to film the scenes of Tommy and Will inside the car. This meant agreeing in advance what shots would be needed, because

Tommy and Will didn't like to be bounced around for shots that weren't going into the movie."

Those shots were worked out digitally, and a rough cut was made.

"We then started filming Tommy and Will in front of blue screens in New York; they were inside this plastic bubble that the physical effects person had built to represent the interior of the 'supercar.' I would say to Tommy and Will, 'We're now filming this angle. It starts here and we're gonna have our camera moving here. We're going to have to rotate the bubble and you just talk, because we're just gonna film the part where the supercar goes up on the wall.' "

The backgrounds were, amazingly, not real, but a one-sixth scale model, and both the LTD and the supercar were computer-generated.

"Afterwards," Brevig concluded, "we composited those shots of Tommy and Will into the computer-graphics shots of the Ford LTD and the 'supercar,' before in turn compositing that image into the tunnel sequence, filmed here at [Industrial Light and Magic]."

It was an incredible piece of work, but an example of the way man and computer interacted in this film, and the way all manner of effects became fully integrated into the story—as opposed to having the story revolve around them.

Sometimes the effects were very basic, as at the film's climax, where a regurgitated Kay lands next to Jay, and the pair of them are covered in alien goo, a scene that took three long, messy days to film.

"That goo was made of methacellulose," Will explained, "with something mixed in and then they would drop some noodles and stuff in to make it fleshy. It got in your ears and nose and hair, twelve hours a day for three days. But the thing that makes Barry such a great director is that he never allows you to be out there by yourself, he put himself in the position to be slimed as well, just so that he could experience what his actors were going through."

(Sonnenfeld's recollection had rather more to do with Will chasing and tackling him, then covering him in the goo.)

When it was all in the can, though, they had the perfect ending to a very funny film, and one which easily lent itself to the kind of franchise every Hollywood release would love to spawn—the sequel. With Kay having quit the Men in Black to have his memory erased and return to a normal life, Dr. Laurel Weaver (Fiorentino's pathologist) had been taken on as Jay's new partner, and between them they'd forged a fresher, hipper style. Still the People in Black, but with a definite fashion consciousness. The scene was set, and even before its release, the follow-up was announced, with Will starring, for 1999.

And there was another industry gearing up, too—the associated products. The betting was that this would be one of the big hits of the summer, and that meant everyone wanted a piece of it. Men in Black action figures and accessories of all kinds hit the stores. Ray Ban sunglasses— admittedly hardly a new product—looked like they'd suddenly become very popular. And far ahead of schedule, the video release of the movie was planned for Thanksgiving, 1997, with heavy television advertising, to take advantage of the busy Christmas market.

It was, as Hollywood had become, a matter of the bottom line and how to maximize it.

That meant, naturally, a soundtrack album, which had become big business. Columbia was putting out the movie, and it just happened that in fall 1996, after completing work on the shooting, Will had signed a recording deal with . . . Columbia Records.

"I just signed a new deal with [them]," Will said. "I've kind of been away from the music for about four years and now with Columbia Records having some smart people working there it feels good to have the opportunity to make some real records."

The first task at hand was to record two songs for the *Men in Black* soundtrack, including the title song; in other words, absolutely no pressure as a comeback. However, if

Will *was* going to record, it did make for a perfectly natural tie-in, and would serve as a great teaser for his own solo album, which would appear later in the year (again, handily, just in time for Christmas). Both the fact that it was Will's return to disc and the hopeful popularity of the movie would carry the song, aimed as a single. At least, that was the plan.

In the event, it worked perfectly. Will couldn't have asked for a happier time. Aided by a video that offered clips from the film as well as one of the funnier dance scenes ever filmed (and which seemed to disprove, even if only just, Jada Pinkett's assertion that "Will can't dance . . . My baby can't dance"), "Men In Black" was one of the top singles of the summer. It became the most played hip-hop song of all time, and went all the way to number one in the *Billboard* charts, as did the sountrack album itself, containing Will's two cuts. Not only was he now a major movie star, Will was back keeping himself in the public eye on two fronts.

It was almost a reversion to the old days, when Will needed to be constantly busy in two different arenas to feel satisfied. And he was going to be busy for a while, putting his new album together.

He was also trying on a new persona, which he'd first referred to in interviews for *Men In Black,* referring to himself as "Big Willie." Given his size, it was apt, and, unlike "Fresh Prince," it was the nickname of an adult. Will Smith was all grown up and ready to prove it.

Everyone might have been predicting success for *Men in Black* on its holiday release, and the huge advertising budget meant that almost everyone in America was ready for it. But nothing was certain until the theaters opened, filled, and the receipts were counted. Until that point, it was a case of holding your breath and hoping for the best.

For completely different reasons, Will scored a direct hit with the critics two summers in a row. Writers had loved *Independence Day* because it didn't try to be anything more than out-and-out adventure; there was no pretension involved. *Men in Black* was also unpretentious, but that didn't mean, in the words of Stuart Klawans, writing in *The Nation*, that it wasn't "the season's smartest, funniest, best pop movie. . . ."

It had everything going for it, in exactly the right proportions. There was witty dialogue (some of which had been rewritten by the actors themselves: When Will the policeman jumped onto a tourist bus in New York, the original line had him apologizing to a group of Japanese tourists. In the final version, thanks to Will, he now said, "It's raining black people in New York"), and at times an underlying sense of pathos. The effects were important, but it was the actors who drove the movie, as Klawans noted: ". . . *Men in Black* is the rare action-comedy that relies on puppetry more than computer animation, and relaxed and self-assured acting more than frenetic camera movement and high body counts."

In *Entertainment Weekly*, Owen Gleiberman called it "a comedy of facetiousness in which facetiousness consumes everything in its path. . . . *Men in Black* combines the anthropomorphic kiddie ghoulishness of the *Star Wars* bar scene with the blasé showbiz hipsterism of *Ghostbusters*," adding that, "It's no surprise that Smith gets most of the good lines, or that he zings them with his inimitably suave timing. Smith's sexiness makes him likable rather than dangerous—it says 'I look so good, I don't even have to be this funny!' " *People* found it a "delightfully droll, offbeat sci-fi comedy." In *Maclean's*, Brian D. Johnson noted that "Built for laughs, not thrills, the movie plays as an affectionate parody of UFO folklore."

It had everything going for it, including audiences. While it was unlikely to find itself sitting atop the all-time highest grosses—outright action films would always outdraw comedies—it certainly did amazing business as the top movie for much of the summer in America, and then Europe as it went into release there in August. The first weekend of its release, over July 4, 1997, it took in $51 million, breaking the record Will had set the year before with *Independence Day.*

Like *Independence Day,* it tapped into the ongoing zeitgeist about aliens, the fascination with other life that might be out there. And as part of that, it was probably inevitable that Will would be asked about his own beliefs.

"Everywhere I go, it's the same thing," he said. "I'm in a restaurant and the waitress will say, 'Will, do you want fries with that, and do you believe in aliens? My sister saw this green light the other night and I told her maybe she should call you to check it out.' I feel like I've entered the Twilight Zone or something. I don't know about the vibe in this country right now, but people seem very excited about the whole idea that there is life out there. [Being] excited is one thing. Meeting someone with pointy ears is another."

But *Men in Black* tipped the whole concept on its head, and by doing so made it completely accessible and . . . human, which is perhaps the hallmark of anything Spielberg has been involved with.

And Spielberg did contribute more than his name to the film.

"Steven had great ideas not only in pre-production," Sonnenfeld explained, "but I would show him stuff in post, and he would say, 'You know, would it be funny it you got an additional shot of Will looking through the window?' I'd say, 'You know what? I don't know, but I'll shoot it because. . . .' Well shit, it's Steven Spielberg. I don't think it's funny, but what the hell. I did it, cut it in, and it was hilarious."

But ultimately, though, *Men in Black* was Will's movie. His might not have been the headlining name, but it was his character that was the real focus, who developed during the running time, who had many of the best lines, and who displayed the bright personality.

Independence Day made him A-list; *Men in Black* firmly cemented his status there. It showed that he not only had the pulling power, but the charisma—a rarely used word, but one that was all too true in his case—to sustain it all. The numbers on his last three movies had been very impressive, enough to make him the most popular African-American actor on the screen.

In and of itself, it was a strange situation, but one which spoke volumes about the United States. There were plenty of other black actors who were dramatically better, people like Denzel Washington, Laurence Fishburne, and Samuel L. Jackson, just to name a few. But the names who were considered bankable, in Hollywood terms, could be counted on the fingers of one hand.

Obviously, a big part of Will's popularity came because of the movies he'd been involved with. But a bigger factor was that his three biggest films had all shown him with a comic edge, and one that wasn't intimidating or "in your face." The biggest secret to Will's success, as he understood, was that he wasn't threatening to middle America. There was nothing deliberate about it; it wasn't something he'd sought out. It was simply Will being Will. Though the attitude towards him and the respect he received had altered as his star continued to ascend, that natural warmth and goofiness were his real weapons. He was, by his very nature, the good guy.

CHAPTER TEN

WITH the completion of *Men in Black,* there still wasn't any time for Will to ease up and take a real vacation—not that he'd have wanted one, anyway. At the top of his agenda was his album, marking Will's return to hip-hop. Following that there'd be two more films back-to-back, *Enemy of the State,* with Will taking the role that Tom Cruise had reportedly rejected; and a remake of the old television show "The Wild, Wild West," which would star Will and George Clooney, and be directed by Barry Sonnenfeld. When he was done with those, the sequel to *Bad Boys,* provisionally titled *Bad Around The World* was due to be filmed. Once all those were out of the way, Will would be working with Sonnenfeld once more, on the sequel to *Men in Black.*

It was an extraordinarily full dance card, one which would take him all the way through until late 1998. Any actor would have loved to have been in a similar position, in demand, contracts signed and sealed, and the money waiting in the bank.

With three huge hits under his belt, Will's price had skyrocketed. When he signed for *Men in Black,* before *Independence Day* was released, he was paid $5 million. It was hardly spare change, but by Hollywood standards, it certainly wasn't top star money. Two years later, putting his name on the contract for the sequel, that had all changed. Reportedly, the figure had now swollen to $12 million—and they were glad to have him at that price.

One person who never had to pay to see him, though,

was Jada Pinkett. The relationship that had appeared to begin on the rebound continued to grow stronger and stronger. She'd become part of his life, and he of hers. She had her star, and he had his, as her popularity continued to grow. *Set It Off* did well critically, even if it was never likely to be a major box-office smash. People knew the elfin Jada; at twenty-five, she had a very strong future.

After dating for a year, it became apparent to Jada and to Will that there was very little sense in not living together. She'd come to know and love Trey, whom Will had at the Thousand Oaks house as often as he could. There she was, an hour away in Los Angeles, with all her possessions in her condo, when there was plenty of room at Will's. As it was, they spent all their free time together, anyway.

The house was amply protected by four Rottweilers. Will had been given two of them on-air during "The Tonight Show" by Jay Leno, and he'd liked the breed so much that he'd acquired another pair.

The relationship Will and Jada shared was completely committed. Neither of them could find a reason for her not to move in. But at the same time, neither of them was thinking about marriage.

"I'm not one of those women who's dying to get married," Jada explained. "I don't romanticize about marriage. Marriage is some work. Everybody's talking about me and Will getting married, and it's, like, he just got *divorced*. There's some things that we need to figure out as far as why that happened, because if I get married, there ain't going to be no divorce. The only reason I would get married is if I'm ready to have kids. No time before that. Will and I are just enjoying this life that we have together. It's fine like this."

That she loved Will was obvious, as were his feelings for her.

"She just understands life . . . the parameters of living. She's very, very in touch with her emotions, which allows me to be in touch with mine. She helps me deal with everything that I have to deal with. She makes everything okay, no matter how difficult it gets. She always has something kind to say or a warm hug or she'll cry with you if you feel like crying. But she'll also punch somebody in the face if they do something to me.''

When she moved into Thousand Oaks, Jada and Will were able to take a little time to nest together. No matter how much time she'd spent there in the past, this was a new and different feeling. Before, she'd had her own place she could retreat to. Now this was her home, too, and that was bound to require a few adjustments.

This was a house with a cook, with staff, more Fresh Prince than suburban Philly. But all the trappings in the world wouldn't stop Will spoiling Jada whenever the mood took him, even taking over the kitchen himself to make regular, down-home food for the two of them.

''He cooks apple and banana pancakes, fried chicken, sweet potato pies,'' said Jada.

And when he was gone—which would be a lot of the time, given his filming schedule—the two of them would talk often, sometimes as much as five times a day.

Settling down like that didn't mean that Jada was less inclined to shock people. There would still be the very close-fitting and revealing dresses that had become almost a trademark of her public appearances, including one particularly sexy number she wore when she and Will attended the Tyson-Holyfield fight.

''I knew people would be looking at that dress,'' she admitted. ''I was also trying to teach Will a lesson. It's like, 'I'm yours no matter what I wear or where I am.' He wanted me to wear the dress, but he didn't want to deal with all the nuisance of people looking and talking. Then I wore it and he felt like a king. He thought he was the *man*!''

Once Jada—or ''Miss Jada'' as Will tended to refer to her—settled into the house, life seemed as good as it could get for Will. He had his girl, he had his son over as often as he could. He had golf to occupy what little free time there was.

And for work, during the late 1996 and early 1997, he had his album to think about. His two tracks on the *Men In Black* soundtrack had been a toe in the water, and reaction had been better than he could have hoped for after so long away from music. (In fact, the second track, "Just Cruisin'," was released as a single in Britain in December 1997, well after the movie, and went straight into the singles charts.) And the tone of rap, which had turned him off for so long with its references to guns, violence, and misogyny, had altered again, lightening in both sound and content. The biggest artist of the year, beyond any debate, was Puff Daddy, whose music was really just pop with a hip-hop beat—something Will could relate to. If any time was perfect for him to return to the recording studio, this was it.

"The dance stuff definitely has a hold on the bodies and minds of the fans right now," commented Selwyn Syfu Hinds, editor of *The Source*. "With Mase and Puffy topping the charts and leading the rush to the dance floor, it's an atmosphere set up for Will to come back. . . ."

More than anything, he didn't want to be seen as a movie star cashing in on his fame with an album. Anyone even slightly familiar with his career would know that wasn't the case, but many wouldn't make the association. He was coming back as himself, not the Fresh Prince, but as Big Willie. The Prince would be inside him, but this time it would be the grown man talking.

It was vitally important to Will that the album, as with anything he'd been involved in, wasn't just thrown together and rushed onto the market. Every phase of it was important to him, and he spent a long time working on the raps.

"There's nothing more unappealing than somebody with a mike standing up, abusing their right to free speech and saying the dumbest speech you ever heard," he said. "A couple artists stand out—Nas, the Fugees—but for the most part, it's basically uneducated people with a podium." That, he thought, was true throughout hip-hop. "When I think of gangsta rap, I think of people who *think* they're doing what Tupac and Biggie were doing, but intellectually, spiritually, they're fallin' short of the mark. When Tupac made the song "Wonder Why They Call U Bytch," that was brilliant. He explained in the record like he was fifteen years deep into a psychological practice, like he had his Ph.D. in psychology, you know. . . . That was the thing about Tupac and Biggie: They were prophets. They were intellectually light-years ahead of everyone else. It's *not* just a coupla niggas cursing about hating people."

The album, appropriately called *Big Willie Style* would include the *Men in Black* theme (with its sample from Patrice Rushen's single "Forget Me Nots"), which would win a Grammy for Best Solo Rap Performance in March 1998. It would also contain something to show that Will hadn't completely turned his back on the past.

Three tracks would have production by Jeff Townes, a couple of them even featuring him scratching on the decks, recorded at the studio in Philadelphia that he now owned. It was only fitting that Jeff and Will should work together again; it offered a measure of continuity to what Will was doing.

And what exactly is a big willie?

"When you say someone is a willie, it means they're at the top of what they do," explained Will. "Michael Jordan is a big willie in basketball. Donald Trump is a big willie in business. I consider myself a big willie in the world of rap. And it kind of works out, because my name is Willie."

For the most part, though, he worked closer to what was home these days, Los Angeles, with the team of Poke and Tone producing. Of course he brought in guests, like Camp Lo and Coko, even Left Eye from TLC. But the biggest surprise was Larry Blackmon and Cameo, who hadn't really been heard of in the better part of a decade. In the mid-eighties, their singles "Candy" and "Word Up" had been quite influential in urban contemporary music, crossing over into the mainstream charts. Obviously their particular style of funk had been an influence on Will, enough to get them on his own album for the track "Candy," which sampled from Cameo's song of the same name. But there was also one of the most underrated singers of recent times, Trey Lorenz, who'd initially become known working as one of Mariah Carey's backup singers.

A glance at the credits showed that Will was becoming more involved in every aspect of the making of a record. He co-produced a number of tracks, and had partial writing credits on every piece. His own managers, James Lassiter and Benny Medina—the same Benny Medina who'd brought him to television—were among the record's executive producers, and the whole thing had been created under the auspices of Will Smith Enterprises.

Musically it wasn't as groundbreaking as some of the early Fresh Prince and Jazzy Jeff releases, but that was only to be expected. Discovery can often come through experimentation, not being quite sure how you want to express yourself, and fumbling. These days Will was older, and had a much greater sense of himself and his place in the world. And for the most part he was working with seasoned veterans of the music business, who wanted to create something *good,* rather than pushing the envelope.

For all that, it wasn't complacent, by any means; it was definitely Will. There was a sense of fun about the whole album, as if his intention had been to have fun making it, and that communicated itself well. There were messages to put across, such as the plea to stop the East Coast–West Coast violence on "Yes Yes Y'All." If there was anything to be communicated, it was that rap could be fun, as it had been in the old school days—back when it had really meant everything to a young Willard C. Smith in suburban Philadelphia—and he wanted to celebrate that sense.

"Rap got away from the essence," he said. "The essence of rap was always about partying and having fun. The best rapper was the one that could rock the crowd. How well you shot a gun wasn't part of the criteria."

Evidently a lot of other people wanted a return to the old school, as the record entered the *Billboard* charts at thirty-one. And it was a celebration at MTV, too, which gave him "Will TV" on November 30, to play the Top 100 Jams, as well as airing a show of his greatest MTV moments.

Big Willie Style didn't seem to sell too well initially, but there was no cause for alarm. Just because it didn't enter the charts at number one didn't mean things weren't going to happen. Its first single, "Gettin' Jiggy Wit It," *was* a number one hit on the *Billboard* pop charts, and quickly became part of the language among blacks and whites all across America. The album moved like a rocket, selling more than two million copies, and spending weeks hovering in the top fifty. "Gettin' Jiggy Wit It" proved to be an international hit, sending Will into the upper reaches of the Top Ten in Britain.

Once again he'd shown that he had the Midas touch, only instead of gold, it seemed to be platinum. And while he might not have been mining socially conscious seams in his lyrics, that didn't worry him. What he was doing, he was doing very successfully indeed. *Big Willie Style* had been something of a comeback after a long time away from music, and things couldn't have gone better. No one accused him of cashing in on his new fame as a movie star. That wouldn't have worked, anyway; Will could simply have pointed to his history.

He had a few inspirations to teach through his music, or through anything he did.

"I always wanted to be an entertainer," he reiterated in *Vibe* in 1998. "My instincts have always been comedic. Rap music was just one of the things that I chose to do to entertain people."

He'd learned what worked for him, and he was sticking to it. It was a lesson he'd learned early, when his grandmother found his first book of rap lyrics, back when Will was twelve and trying to be adult.

"Dear Will," she'd written, "Truly intelligent people do not have to use this type of language to express themselves. Why don't you show the world that you are as smart as we all think you are?"

And that was exactly what he'd done. He was still doing it. But even when he was souding streetwise, behind it all Will was speaking with perfect grammar, and insisted that Trey, and even Jada do so as well. ("Captain Correction" was one of her nicknames for him.)

The fact that *Big Willie Style* sold so well simply confirmed that Will Smith had managed to transcend all genres and pigeonholes. People liked him, and they liked what he did. He followed his gut instincts, and they were perfectly in tune with America—indeed, with the world. He might live behind gates in a mansion called Hacienda de Norte, but he understood what made the average person tick—he was the average man himself. Certain things might make him aware every single day that he was black, but most people didn't see him that way. He'd gone beyond color to be one of them.

More than that, he'd established himself as a force, even as a new generation of artists rode the charts. With Jazzy Jeff, a decade before, he'd been one of the pioneers, among the first to score hits with rap music. That he could do it again, ten years later, said a great deal, both about Will Smith, and his music. His finger remained very firmly on the pulse.

More than just looking out for himself, through Will Smith Enterprises he was developing other talent. His first real protege was Tatyana Ali, who'd been his co-star in "The Fresh Prince of Bel Air." He took an active role in her first album, and when it turned into a success in 1998, a certain amount of the credit had to go to Will. He was showing himself to be a master at putting together records that he knew people would want to hear, and discovering talent.

But it would be too much to hope that Will could focus completely on one—or even two—things. Although he wasn't acting in any movies at the time, they weren't far from his mind. Now he was writing one.

He'd kept in mind the lesson Bill Cosby had given him in 1993, the advice to write an episode of his sitcom. Writing—other than raps—was something that hadn't appeared on his resume yet, but that would change when he and Jada sat down and began to hash out an idea for a screenplay.

Love For Sale, as they called it, became the story of a woman who wanted a child, and asked a construction worker to father it. For a fee, he was willing, but later had reservations about the whole deal, which then turned into a romance.

Once they began writing, everything flowed very quickly. Naturally, both of them were more than familiar with the format of screenplays, and over the space of a couple of months—a ludicrously short time—they moved from first draft to finished product.

The question then was what to do with it. The whole process had been fun, but now they had something complete that they felt was good. There was always the option to make it themselves, with Will and Jada in the starring roles. After all, their lives were entwined, so why not their careers as well? The biggest obstacle was time. Studios would have been happy to finance any project with Will in the lead role, but his commitments simply didn't give him the freedom to take on anything else, even through his new production company.

The best answer was to see if anyone else was interested. Of course, their names had cachet in the industry, which certainly helped matters along, and the script was quickly picked up by Universal in April of 1997.

It was the first thing they'd undertaken together, but it wouldn't be the last. By the end of the year they were making their lives into a joint venture.

The first inkling came in November, when the couple announced their engagement, Jada sporting a huge diamond ring that Will had bought for her. According to her, he'd proposed when they were in bed, saying quite simply that he couldn't live without her and wanted to marry her. She, in turn, had quickly answered yes.

Originally they'd wanted a very public ceremony in Los Angeles, but soon that idea was shunted aside for something more private, to be held in Jada's hometown of Baltimore on New Year's Eve.

The ceremony was quite lavish by most standards, although not exactly Hollywood—it was held at Cloisters, a Tudor-style mansion just outside Baltimore. Certainly no expense was spared. Velvet was draped everywhere, gilded magnolia leaves were brought from Virginia, and burgundy calla lilies were imported from New Zealand. Gold floodlight lit the building—Jada had worked with a wedding planner on the event—while smaller lights and maroon ribbons festooned the brickwork. Three hundred candles lit the interior, while exotic flower arrangements filled all the nooks and crannies. It took eight decorators ten hours to complete all the work that Jada wanted to make her wedding day memorable.

Naturally, although people knew that Will and Jada were getting married, they didn't want it to be a public occasion. Instead, there was great secrecy about the entire affair. The guests were all put up in one hotel. When they awoke on New Year's Eve, they received their "instructions"—directions to the Cloisters—and had to hand them to their limo drivers. Will had hired an entire fleet of limousines for the occasion.

The ceremony itself wasn't until eight P.M., but everyone, including bride and groom, was there early. Jada wasn't in the least bit nervous. Originally she'd planned on wearing a duplicate of her grandmother's wedding dress, but with just a week to go to the wedding had changed her mind. She decided on something original, designed by Badgley Mischka—hand-dyed silk velvet.

Will arrived not long after Jada, escorted by some friends and Trey. Like his bride-to-be, he'd gone with clothes by Badgley Mischka.

Trey and the other children led the way down the aisle, after the ceremony had been started by Infinity, a group of *a capella* singers. Then it was Will and Jada, walking down the aisle together—no best man, no one to give the bride way. Both bride and groom had written letters expressing their love for each other, and they read those during the ceremony, as part of their vows. When Jada was finished, Will asked the pastor, "Can I kiss her now?"

And so Will Smith and Jada Pinkett joined their lives, and the party began, with buffet tables laden with poached salmon and smoked turkey. Upstairs, people were dancing as a DJ worked his trade, and even Will was enticed into action, grabbing Trey, jumping on stage to sing "Gettin' Jiggy Wit It." He and Jada stayed until 1 A.M., before heading back to the condo they'd rented by the harbor. They were able to cram a three-day honeymoon into their schedules, flying down to Miami, before work called again. Will had to return to the West Coast to resume the filming of his new movie, *Enemy of the State*.

Obviously, given that Jada had said that the only reason she'd marry was to have children, it seemed likely that they'd be planning offspring soon. Both were young, and although Will had Trey, that didn't stop them wanting to have kids of their own. What neither had anticipated was that it would happen so soon. The engagement had barely been announced when there was another press release, stating that Jada was pregnant.

It was unplanned and unexpected, but certainly not unwanted. Due in the summer of 1998, the idea of a baby was thrilling to them both.

However, as Jada took great pains to point out, that wasn't the reason they were marrying. They hadn't even found out she was pregnant until Will had proposed and she had accepted. The baby was simply the icing on the matrimonial cake.

It all happened as Will was at the tail end of his daily commute into Los Angeles to finish filming *Enemy of the State*, a movie that would put him into very unfamiliar territory. Never before had he attempted a straight thriller. Taking the role that Tom Cruise had reportedly turned down, he was opposite Gene Hackman—once again, pairing himself with the best. The director was Tony Scott, whose credits included *Top Gun, Beverly Hills Cop,* and who'd worked with Hackman before on *Crimson Tide,* where he'd been paired with one of the other leading black actors, Denzel Washington.

Was it a good move for Will? Certainly, after two science-fiction films back-to-back, he needed a change of pace, and one thing he wanted to avoid was being typecast. And he'd always said he wanted to keep challenging himself, to take some unexpected roles and continually surprise people. This, with its political bent—and its inevitable action—would certainly do that. But was it coming a little too late? Had *Bad Boys, Independence Day,* and *Men in Black* established a public perception of Will Smith—someone loveable and slightly goofy, capable of action, a man with a good heart, and a bit of a comic—and tied him to it?

It seemed quite possible. Those were the films that had elevated him to superstar status, and that had given him a household name. If he could convoncingly break out of that, and if *Enemy of the State* was financially successful, then the sky would be the limit for Will in the future. He'd have proved he could do anything.

Enemy of the State had a troubled history, however. Early drafts of the script had been rejected by director Scott, Hackman, and Disney.

However, with work, that altered. Will's character became a young, successful lawyer who suddenly found his life a mess thanks to an unstable agent in the National Security Agency. On the run, he found himself pursued by government agents, and aided by a journalist (Jason Lee), and a former spy (Hackman).

The fact that it would be much heavier and meatier than most of Will's previous films, and certainly the ones that had brought him major success, meant that he was now willing to take even more chances. By the time *Enemy of the State* appeared, in November 1998, he'd been away from the movie screens for well over a year. He could come back with something fresh and different, something more adult.

In a very quiet way, too, he'd added another string to his bow. When the Million Man March had first been mentioned, the idea had interested him.

Put forward by Louis Farrakhan, head of the Nation of Islam, it was meant as an event for black men in America. They would come together in Washington D.C. in 1996, partly as a celebration of existence, and partly to counter the negative media image of black males.

These were responsible, thoughtful people, the type rarely read about in the newspapers or seen on television, but more representative of the black majority. As a way of acknowledging themselves and letting white America know of their existence, it was ideal.

Filmmaker Spike Lee was fascinated, too, so much so that he wanted to make a documentary following a group of men on their journey to the march, and during it. It was the kind of small project no studio would be interested in financing, even with Lee's reputation, and that meant he needed backers.

Will had frequently expressed interest in working with him, and now he had his first chance, albeit not in the way that many people had hoped. Will became one of the financial angels of Lee's *Get on the Bus,* which appeared in a few theaters some months after the march.

And Will himself was in Washington on that day. It was important to him to attend, and his being there was a very rare political gesture.

But his involvement with Spike Lee on this project would lead to more talks between them, and discussions about a possible future project. One of Lee's great loves was basketball, a game Will loved too, and which, with his height, he was able to play convincingly. Lee had been considering a film about the 1994/95 Houston Rockets season, (when, to the surprise of many, they were the top team in the NBA) and cast Will as one of the leads. There was no date set for filming, and no firm backing from the studio, but it remained something they both wanted to do in the future.

Would it happen? Possibly. Lee's last couple of big films, *Clockers* and *Girl 6,* hadn't been particularly successful, either critically or financially. But he had a way of bouncing back. And with a commitment from a major name like Will, anything was possible. Although it would mean Will would be working for far less than his usual salary (Lee wouldn't have the money to match the $12 million Will was reportedly receiving for the sequel to *Men in Black*), this was one of the directors Will really wanted to work with. Very few black directors had managed to make any kind of mark in the business, and Lee was still the biggest name among them all. Working with him would be an artistic validation for Will.

But he was so heavily booked that time would be as much a factor as anything else. In April 1998 he was due to begin work on *The Wild, Wild West,* co-starring Kevin Kline, followed by *Men in Black II,* both of which were scheduled for 1999 releases.

As to *Bad Around The World,* the sequel to *Bad Boys,* it seemed to be undergoing script problems. There were plans to shoot in Miami and London, but the only immediate space on Will's calendar was the beginning of 1998. It looked uncertain as to whether everything would be ready by then.

Somewhere in there, too, he'd have to start thinking about another record. But all it meant was that life for Will Smith was very, very good. He was in constant demand, he was rich again, and he was very happy.

The biggest event, bigger even than his wedding, happened in July 1998, when Jada gave birth to Jaden Christopher Syre. It was noticeable that the pair kept details of the birth to a minimum. They both spent enough time in the public eye because of their careers not to want to have the camera and journalists invade their private lives too—especially in something as intimate as this. Jada had said of her marriage that "I refuse to let the public impose their response on us," and it was equally truth of the birth of their son.

Jaden stood as a symbol of their love and commitment to each other, a love that was sometimes inspirational to others.

"One of the things I love most about sharing my life with Will is that so many black women approach me and say, 'You just don't know how much hope, how much faith you've given me. I hope that I can love the same way, and I just wish you all the luck in the world with your relationship.' I love the idea that black women feel like love is alive in the air."

It was very much alive—and bouncing, gurgling, and sometimes crying—for Will and Jada. Will had been down this road before, with Trey; but for Jada it would be an entirely new adventure, one that she'd share with her husband.

Inevitably, the birth would alter their lives. They both had very active careers, but still wanted to make as much time as possible for the new baby. That meant juggling any number of things. Of course, they were luckier than most couples, in that they could afford a staff and a nanny if they needed one. It would make day-to-day living a little easier, most definitely. But Will and Jada would still have the responsibility of raising Jaden. And, as Will knew from his ongoing involvement with Trey, that was a heavy responsibility.

CHAPTER ELEVEN

EVEN before his thirtieth birthday, Will had managed to occupy a unique niche in entertainment. He'd become the first person to have had huge careers in music, television, and films. Curiously, it had never happened before. The closest had perhaps been Elvis Presley and Frank Sinatra, who had both had many, many hit records and popular films but neither had taken roles in television series, let alone starred in them.

Since Will, Queen Latifah had established herself in all three fields, but with nothing like Will's presence. And that left him alone at the top of the heap.

All along he'd felt compelled to excel, to be the best at whatever he did, and he'd proved that he was. He'd made himself unassailable, and the fact that he'd been a nice guy throughout it all only added to his luster.

"The thing I've learned in Holloywood is that I don't know what my limits are," he explained. "I have no idea what my limits are. And I say this to my friends a lot, you know, jokin'. But I'm really serious. I feel like I could be the President of the United States. I feel like I could win! People laugh, but I swear, I'm not just sayin' this to be funny. . . . I believe that if I set my mind to it, within the next fifteen years, I would be the President of the United States."

Maybe it was an exaggeration, but maybe not. Will, it seemed, had the power to be succcessful at anything that he wanted. He'd learned from the mistakes he made when he was young, enjoying the first flush of riches. He might have blown it all then, but in coming back, he showed remarkable fortitude. Very few men of twenty could lose everything, then grit their teeth and start all over again, from nothing, and scale even greater heights.

Essentially, everything he'd done was a testament to his ability and his willpower. Having had an idea of what he could do, he wasn't about to stop until he'd fulfilled everything he knew was inside him. Being a self-confessed workaholic helped, having the energy for project after project—often two at the same time. But drive alone didn't equate to success. His self-confidence and that overriding need to be the best made all the difference.

With the ups came the downs; that was inevitable. But even then he managed to make the most of them. His marriage to Sheree Zampano didn't work, but from it came Trey, who, with Jada, is one of the central lights of his life. When Will describes himself as home-loving, it's the truth, not Hollywood hype washing over the scandals of a star. Even his great acting failure, not kissing another man in *Six Degrees of Separation*, was a lesson to him. Later, he regretted it, and it gave him an understanding of himself, both as a man and an actor, one which helped him become better as both.

These days the "Fresh Prince" might be more part of his past than his present, but even he realizes that person is still inside him. There are times he'll peek through and make himself known, even if he doesn't define Will Smith any more.

"The Fresh Prince can come over for dinner," he said wryly, "but he's got to go home again."

And all the fame and fortune hasn't gone to his head. The grounding he received from his parents has stayed with him. In his position, many men would feel as if they could do no wrong. Instead, Will's attitude is much more down to earth.

"I'd love to say that I'm brilliant, that I'm the Second Coming. The real answer is that I'm blessed. I throw 'em up from wherever I am and they just keep going in."

He'd been lucky, but luck was one factor everyone relies on. Still, without a bedrock of natural talent, he wouldn't have got that far.

"Will is one of those fated people," said Benny Medina, "one of those destined people, somebody who somehow makes sure he hits the mark he's supposed to. . . . He has a likability factor that I haven't seen in many people in this business. And he is hungry. With those qualities, you don't anticipate any boundaries."

But he has begun to learn a few lessons about slowing down. In spring 1997, he and Jada went to visit Eddie Murphy on his farm in New York. Will was full of everything that was happening to him, the deals, the money, everyone after his services. Murphy, sitting out in the sunshine in a golf cart, playing a guitar, looked at him and said,

"It ain't no race. You're twenty-eight years old. What are you running for?"

"I'm looking at him, sitting in his cart with that guitar," Will recalled. "He just looked so happy with those little kids. And I said, 'That's what I want.' "

It was definite food for thought, the kind of moment to jerk his head firmly back out of the clouds and back to this planet. Will is a very rich man. This time around, he's done things right. His younger brother, Harry, is now his business manager, so there's no danger of him ever being cheated by unscupulous managers—as has happened to so many actors and musicians in the past. His desire for wild spending died in 1989 with that huge bill from the IRS. He has, really, more than he could ever spend. Now that he and Jada are parents, it's possible that he will finally learn to slow down a little, and enjoy the life that he has around him. These days he can, quite literally, pick and choose the projects he wishes to be involved with; he's become that big A-list star. But one thing is certain, he wants to continue in films.

"I enjoy making movies. It allows you to be someone different every time you step up to the camera. You know, television is a medium designed for mediocrity, whereas when you're making a film, you have more of an opportunity to achieve aesthetic perfection, or as close to that as you can get. You just have time to work on it all.''

That's a true statement, to an extent. Any actor is still confined by the director, and by budget and shooting time. But the relative freedom of films—as opposed to television—was always bound to appeal to Will's desire to be the best. There *is* the time to reshoot scenes until they're just right.

Given Will's goals, it's perhaps surprising that he's shown no inclination towards directing a film. It would, after all, offer him the ultimate control, the chance to shape things the way he wanted, in his own vision.

There are a couple of possibilities as to why he hasn't pursued this. The first is simply time. His calendar has been so full—and so lucratively full—that he simply hasn't had a second to think of anything in films beyond acting, and he certainly wouldn't make anywhere near the money as a director that he does as an actor. As an actor, he puts three months into the filming of a project, then moves on. As a director, each film would be a year of his life, working not only on the shoot, but pre- and post-production.

Second, he might just not feel ready yet. Many actors have made the transition to director, and, in many ways, moving from one side of the camera to the other is a perfectly natural progression. But it requires quite a bit of technical expertise to be done properly. Novices often rely on their cinematographers to carry the load. Were Will to move into directing a feature, his personality is such that he'd need to take the whole load on himself, which would mean a great deal of study beforehand. And while he's already learned a lot, there's undoubtedly still a long way to go.

But with his love of a challenge, it's almost certainly a thought that's come into his head from time to time. He's done everything else, so why not this? And every move he's made so far—rapper to TV star to movie star to screenwriter—has been successful; why shouldn't another one work just as well?

It might, in time. But the stakes would be very high. As a star he's paid a lot of money to do one thing very well. As a director he'd be paid a lot less to be responsible not only for the stars, but everything, including the money invested in the film.

So probably the time will come when he'll direct, but not for several years yet. Apart from anything else, he's seen the general fate of black directors in Hollywood—they haven't been generally warmly welcomed into the fraternity. A black actor turned director would have many similar problems, although the clout that his name has would soften many of them.

Before all that, though, there are the Spike Lees and John Singletons, directors he wants to work with. Acting is far from a dead end at the moment for Will. And it won't be that way until he's played every type of character, and shown himself as multi-faceted.

One thing he's never lacked is self-confidence. He's always had a strong idea of his abilities and innate talent, and the knowledge that he's always been a quick learner. His rapid progress as an actor in ''The Fresh Prince of Bel Air'' is testament to that. And though he'll readily admit that it's the charm that helped him get things in the first place, he's always been able to back that up and deliver the goods when it came time.

And self-confidence has been a major trait of almost all the characters he's played, whether on television or on-screen. The Fresh Prince himself had plenty of sass, was streetwise and hip (in a way that Will himself never quite was, but still managed to put across convincingly). Paul Poitier was a young man of infinite charm, who was able to convince others of his false identity because he approached things as if they couldn't be anything but true, utterly certain that these people would ''help'' him. Mike Lowery had complete faith in his ability as a cop, and in himself as a person. Steven Hiller never doubted that he, the Marine Corps, and Earth would triumph over the aliens. And Agent Jay, bemused though he was by the new world he'd become part of, still managed to take it all in stride—always confident that his ability would see him through—

In other words, his biggest roles have essentially been mirrors of Will's own personality, in one form or another. Even as the villain in *Six Degrees of Separation* he had to present a side that was pleasant without being unctuous, to turn the charm on and come across as the good, nice young man—which was the easy part.

So in many ways, he hasn't been called upon to stretch himself too far yet. With Will, what we've seen is what there is. His image is as a good, pleasant, slightly goofy person, someone not from the hard streets, but the much softer suburbs. And for once, the image truly does echo the reality.

He studied the careers of those people who'd made a successful move from television to film, and there weren't many of them—Tom Hanks, Eddie Murphy, and Jim Carrey. He carefully looked at what they had in common.

"It came down to a couple of basic elements," Will explained. "They were regular guys. You looked at them and you felt like you had a great sense of who this person was when they were at home with their wife and kids. Just a regular guy. And I thought, 'Well, hell, why can't the next regular guy be me?' "

It is. Will is, quite simply, a nice guy.

There have never been any rumors of tantrums on the set from him. And beyond the "Michael Bay Encyclical,"—which was always more joke than anything—there is nothing to indicate any type of star behavior. He's a working man who happens to have been very lucky. He's stayed focused and sharp in everything he's done. He's worked hard, and stayed completely out of trouble. Neither drugs nor violence are ever mentioned in the same breath as Will Smith.

His intention has always been to play positive roles, and he's done that, with the possible exception of Paul Poitier.

And in doing that, as well as the exemplary way he's lived his own life, he's come across as an ideal role model. This is one of the reasons that Nickelodeon, the childrens' television channel, honored him with the 1997 Hall Of Fame Award, for his work and himself. He also received a nomination in the 1996 NAACP Image Awards for his work on ''The Fresh Prince Of Bel Air'' (the show itself also received a nomination).

It's all perfectly genuine, and can be traced back to the influence his parents have had on him, an influence that still pervades everything Will does.

''The only real litmus test in the work that I do and the way that I behave is that I want my Mom to not be embarrassed by it when she's at work,'' he acknowledged, ''because I don't want her to feel embarrassed if my song comes on the radio, or if a lot of people see a movie I'm in. I just don't want to get a spanking.''

That a grown man would have so much feeling and respect for the opinion of his parents says a great deal about Will as a man. The fact that he cares means he hasn't lost touch with who he really is, and at this stage is never likely to.

He's a man with the kind of charisma given to very few, as producer Jerry Bruckheimer pointed out.

''Certain actors have what it takes to be a movie star and it's God-given. The [Tom] Cruise kind of guys, you want to watch them over and over again. Will's there. This is just the beginning.''

But Will also understands that, for all the charisma, it requires a very strong work ethic. Even back in Philly, when he was working with Jazzy Jeff, ''we knew that we had to be practicing while the other guys were eating. We had to be practicing while the other guys were sleeping. We went to school and we practiced, and that was it. People see successful people, and they always think that their success must be because somebody liked them or gave them preferential treatment. . . . But the bottom line is, how hard are you willing to work?''

It's perhaps hard to see how he could get much bigger. Already on the A-list, very few actors get more money for a role than him. To rise higher would put him up with the industry's real heavyweights, the Schwarzeneggers and Willises, probably even higher than Cruise.

For someone who was touted as the next Eddie Murphy at the beginning of the decade, he's come a long, long way. He showed he had everything Murphy had, but also another dimension. It's also worth considering that he's only made six films, of which only four really show him properly. To establish the reputation Will has shows the kind of presence he projects onscreen.

Yes, he's become a huge crossover, maybe even more popular with white fans than black, but to *define* him as a crossover star reduces his impact to one of race. At the end of the day, Will is a star, period, and there should be no mention of race, creed, or color.

However, he might well have an impact on African-American actors following in his footsteps.

''He won't be able to do every movie,'' observed casting director Billy Hopkins. ''But producers will think, 'We'll find the next Will Smith.' So at least a few other black actors will get a shot.''

Maybe the best way to look at Will is how he sees himself.

''I'm fun for everybody,'' he told reporters. That's exactly what he's been, and it's what he'll continue to be. He can't help it: Big Willie is Big Fun.

FiLMS, TELEViSiON, ALBUMS...

FILMS

WHERE THE DAY TAKES YOU
(1992)
Dermot Mulroney . . . King
Lara Flynn Boyle . . . Heather
Ricki Lake . . . Brenda
Will Smith . . . Manny

Marc Rocco . . . Director

MADE IN AMERICA
(1993)
Whoopi Goldberg . . . Sarah Matthews
Ted Danson . . . Hal Jackson
Will Smith . . . Teacake Walters
Nia Long . . . Zora Matthews

Richard Benjamin . . . Director

SIX DEGREES OF SEPARATION
(1993)
Stockard Channing . . . Ouisa Kittredge
Donald Sutherland . . . Flan Kittredge
Will Smith . . . Paul
Mary Beth Hurt . . . Kitty

Fred Schepisi . . . Director

BAD BOYS
(1995)
Will Smith . . . Mike Lowrey
Martin Lawrence . . . Marcus Burnett
Tea Leoni . . . Julie Mott
Marg Helgenberger . . . Alison Sinclair

Michael Bay . . . Director

INDEPENDENCE DAY
(1996)
Will Smith . . . Captain Steven Hiller
Bill Pullman . . . President Whitmore
Jeff Goldblum . . . David Levinson
Vivica A. Fox . . . Jasmine Dubro

Roland Emmerich . . . Director

MEN IN BLACK

Will Smith . . . Agent Jay
Tommy Lee Jones . . . Agent Kay
Linda Fiorentino . . . Laurel
Vincent D'Onforio . . . Edgar

Barry Sonnenfeld . . . Director

ENEMY OF THE STATE
(1998)
Will Smith . . . Robert Dean
Jon Voight . . . Reynolds
Gene Hackman . . . Brill
Jason Lee . . . Zavitz

Tony Scott . . . Director

TELEVISION

"THE FRESH PRINCE OF BEL AIR"
(1990–1996)
Will Smith . . . Will Smith
James Avery . . . Philip Banks
Janet Hubert-Whitten . . . Vivian Banks (1990–1993)
Daphne Reid . . . Vivian Banks (1993–1996)
Alfonso Ribiero . . . Carlton Banks
Karyn Parsons . . . Hilary Banks
Tatyana Ali . . . Ashley Banks

ALBUM DISCOGRAPHY

D.J. JAZZY JEFF AND THE FRESH PRINCE
Rock the House (1987, Jive)
He's the DJ, I'm the Rapper (1988, Jive)
And in This Corner (1989, Jive)
Homebase (1991, Jive)

Code Red (1993, Jive)
Greatest Hits (1998, Jive)

WILL SMITH
Big Willie Style (1997, Columbia)

In an extraordinary book that transcends sports biography, Bob Greene takes the reader along with Jordan over two seasons with the Chicago Bulls, during glorious championship surges and trying personal moments. With rare insight, Greene reveals the person inside the icon: a man who makes millions but cannot go for a quiet walk around the block without getting mobbed, a man who competes ferociously on the court, but who performs some of his most remarkable and unexpected feats away from the limelight.

HANG TIME

BOB GREENE

"Jordan seems to open up more to Greene than anybody."

—Mike Lupica, New York *Daily News*

Get the sizzling inside story on the hot
young star of song and screen

SITTIN' ON TOP OF THE WORLD
ANNA LOUISE GOLDEN

Named one of the "21 hottest stars under 21" by *Teen
People* magazine, Brandy, the chart-topping singer and
star of TV's *Moesha*, is one of today's hottest young
talents—a bright, headstrong woman who handles the
hurdles of stardom with major maturity, while enjoying life like an ordinary teenager (she talks for hours
on the phone, shops up a storm, and *loves* McDonald's
french fries!). Get the 411 on this award-winning
superstar and her life in front of the camera, in back of
the microphone—and *behind* the scenes.

WITH EIGHT PAGES OF FABULOUS PHOTOS!

BRANDY
Anna Louise Golden
0-312-97055-2___$4.99 U.S.___$6.50 Can.

Publishers Book and Audio Mailing Service
P.O. Box 070059, Staten Island, NY 10307
Please send me the book(s) I have checked above. I am enclosing $_____ (please add
$1.50 for the first book, and $.50 for each additional book to cover postage and handling.
Send check or money order only—no CODs) or charge my VISA, MASTERCARD,
DISCOVER or AMERICAN EXPRESS card.

Card Number_____

Expiration date_____Signature_____

Name_____

Address_____

City_____State/Zip _____
Please allow six weeks for delivery. Prices subject to change without notice. Payment in
U.S. funds only. New York residents add applicable sales tax.   BRANDY 3/99

Meet Hollywood's Coolest
Young Superstar!

MATT DAMON

By Kathleen Tracy

Matt Damon is more than just a handsome heartthrob—he's also a talented actor and screenwriter who took home both a Golden Globe Award and an Oscar for co-writing the movie *Good Will Hunting.* Find out how he made it in Hollywood, what he plans for the future, about his lifelong friendship with Ben Affleck, about his steamy relationships with some of his leading ladies, and much, much more! Includes eight pages of exciting photos.

MATT DAMON
Kathleen Tracy
0-312-96857-4 _____ $4.99 U.S. _____ $6.50 CAN.